LANDMARK COLLECTOR'S LIBRARY

Llanrwst:
the History of a Market Town

Norman Tucker

Picture research: Helen Maurice Jones

LANDMARK COLLECTOR'S LIBRARY

LLANRWST:
the History of a Market Town

Norman Tucker

Picture research: Helen Maurice Jones

Landmark Publishing

Published by

Ashbourne Hall, Cokayne Ave
Ashbourne, Derbyshire DE6 1EJ England
Tel: (01335) 347349 Fax: (01335) 347303
e-mail: landmark@clara.net
web site: www.landmarkpublishing.co.uk

1st edition

ISBN 1 84306 070 1

Printed by CPI, Bookcraft, Midsomer Norton, Bath

Design & reproduction by James Allsopp

Cover captions:
Front cover: Llanrwst Parish Church
Back cover; Top: The bridge and Victoria Hotel
Bottom: A gathering outside the George & Dragon Vaults, 1912
Page 1: Gathering the hay near Llanrwst
Page 3: Detail from a photograph of a procession in 1912 (see also back cover)
Opposite page: The former St Mary's Church

CONTENTS

Publisher's Note

This book consists of a previously unpublished manuscript on the early history of Llanrwst written by the late Norman Tucker. After his death, it was deposited by his son with the Conwy Library & Archive Department. Having recently published his history of Colwyn Bay (augmented with later work by Ivor Wynne Jones), the County Librarian and Archivist, Mrs Rona Aldrich suggested that it would be appropriate to bring the work on Llanrwst to a wider audience.

The book concentrates on the town's early development. It was a period to which Mr Tucker had devoted much of his research, not just on Llanrwst but to a much wider area of North Wales.

In researching illustrations to accompany the manuscript, it seemed a pity to discard so many scenes which covered the life of the town not precisely in the period covered by the text. This book thus combines the two – bringing the story of the town's early development alongside its subsequent growth from a village to the town recognised today. The emphasis of the photographs is on scenes which have changed – the loss of the Town Hall, St Mary's Church and the Victoria Hotel being perhaps the most prominent changes.

As the town enters a new millennium, it is perhaps appropriate to look back at its beginnings as it faces the challenges of the future. We hope that you will find this book a timely record of days gone by in Llanrwst.

Some comments made by Mr Tucker clearly relate to the time of writing and not of today and should be read in that context.

We wish to acknowledge the assistance given by both Conwy and Denbigh Archive Service, plus our thanks to Mr Pattinson for use of his photographs and Mr Eryl Owain for checking the proofs.

Mr Tucker wished to acknowledge the assistance of Mr N R Jones, auctioneer of Llanrwst and Mr Robert Jones (see p. 47)

C L M Porter
Landmark Publishing. Ashbourne 2002

INTRODUCTION

Llanrwst, showing its bridge and two churches; St Mary's, on the left, was built in 1842

From early times a river crossing has been a place of consequence. Llanrwst owes its importance to its position. This was the first place where the River Conwy could be crossed without resorting to a ferry. Long before a bridge was built, a ford existed at this spot. Not only was the Conwy the most important waterway in North Wales but it formed a barrier across all east and west trade and travel.

A factor which affected the destiny of Llanrwst was the tidal reach of the river which allowed craft of reasonable tonnage to come sufficiently near to the town to enable cargoes to be shipped to Conwy.

Tides have their vagaries however. When Mrs Enid Mousedale, who was born in Melin-y-coed and later lived at Bryn Dyffryn, was playing with other children south of the bridge, they were surprised to see the river 'flowing the wrong way'. They followed, until opposite the cottage belonging to Gwydir, they saw the river was 'flowing the right way'. Pennant, c. 1770, asserts that the tide did not flow nearer than Llyn y Graig, a mile and a half below Llanrwst Bridge, where at spring tides boats of twelve tons could venture.

That craft of lesser draught could reach Llanrwst is proved by Gwydir keeping its own boat for fetching guests (and probably merchandise) up river from Conwy. When Viscount Bulkeley needed a tree from Gwydir Woods suitable for a vessel he was having built, Sir Richard Wynn (4th Baronet) was able to provide one which he dispatched 'by boat'. 'Cae llong' (ship field) near the bridge is said to mark the spot where ships were built but nothing indicates the size of the vessel. Conwy Church Register in 1750 contains a reference to Robert Roberts of Llanrwst, 'shipwright'.

The creation of a castle-borough at Conwy by Edward I had repercussions on Llanrwst and Trefriw. Burgesses of Conwy jealous of the privileges conferred on them by King Edward's Charter required 'foreigners', as they described merchants from other towns, to pay tolls. This forced many traders to take their wares to Llanrwst or Trefriw.

Llanrwst's interests lay not seaward but eastward. Roads from other market towns, such as Denbigh and Abergele, as well as the dreary routes from Shropshire across the Hiraethog Moors, converged on Llanrwst Bridge and the town benefited thereby. In direct contrast was the territory to the west; the inhospitable region of the Snowdon peaks – haunt of the fox, the falcon and the polecat. Its wildness can be judged by a memorandum by Maurice Wynn in 1570 in which he notes one of his sheep has been killed by an eagle. From this bleak and barren land came the shepherd and hill farmer on market days, glad to get in touch with Llanrwst's friendly inhabitants.

Because of its bridge Llanrwst was a gathering place of drovers from Anglesey and Leŷn who brought their herds of Welsh Blacks on the first leg of their trek to Barnet Fair. Outside Ruthin is the 'Drovers Arms' a reminder of the Drovers' roads. See page 112 for details of "Welsh Cattle Drovers".

Llanrwst in James I's reign was described by Sir John Wynn as a 'village'. Its importance was not so much its size as its site. As an ancient market town it possessed privileges. Neither market nor fair could be held without Royal grant, or Act of Parliament. As far back as 1328 it was compulsory to publish the date when a market or fair was held. Fairs, while primarily an occasion for buying and selling, were also a likely place for brawls, so the carrying of weapons was prohibited.

To all intents Llanrwst was wholly a Denbighshire town. The river like a barrier separated it from the Caernarvonshire side of the parish. The only dwelling considered eligible for recognition was Tu-hwnt-i'r-bont and its name implies that it was 'the house beyond the bridge'.

Half a mile westward stood lordly Gwydir in haughty isolation, as though disdaining plebian company. Plas Isa (to use the old spelling) also stood apart. John Wynn refers to Plas Isa as 'near Llanrwst'. A similar description was applied to Fron Ganol as recently as 1876.

The pattern of the town's development can be traced even today. It reached out to the friendly market towns to the east. From the outset Llanrwst was a compact little place which clustered around its church and bridge. The houses were grouped in cosy neighbourliness about the Market Square. In the centre was a small eminence known as Bryn y Boten which may, in distant days, have held a stockade to protect the river crossing. Beyond lay the great market towns of Oswestry and Shrewsbury, hungry for Welsh wool, and Smithfield even hungrier for Welsh Blacks to be transformed (ironically) into the roast beef of Old England.

Wool played an important part in the development of the town. The trade could probably be traced to the example of the Cistercians in the Abbey of Aberconwy at Maenan some three miles to the north. They were agriculturists and would have encouraged the rearing of sheep in the lush meadows and hilly slopes of the valley.

The monks, in addition to manufacturing habits from undyed wool, which earned for them the name of the White Monks, traded in wool. While the abbey was still at Conwy the

King issued a safe conduct to Chester to a merchant named de Podio whose men were carrying 20 sacks of wool bought from the Abbot of Aberconwy in 1277.

Trade was not restricted to the sale of wool. As a cottage industry spinning, carding and weaving were extensively carried on. A prosperous farmer could own his own loom. Much of the homespun produced was of rough texture but it was in demand particularly when hard wear was required. It was even exported overseas. Buyers came to the July fair at Llanrwst which was the principle mart serving English trade. The wool was dyed from colours extracted from lichen. A small building south of the bridge still goes by the name of the dye-house. Cloth known as 'Welsh cottons' was in demand; also a kind of lindsey-woolsey named 'stuff'. Welsh frieze, a coarse woollen cloth with a nap on one side, was popular for its hard-wearing quality.

E Hude Hall, c. 1810, writes that within the township of Gwydir 'much woollen yarn is spun and woven into a chequered stuff dyed at home of which the chief part is sold at Llanrwst markets and fairs.'

When A G Bradley visited Llanrwst early this century on a fair day, he found it crowded with traps and carts. It was, he asserts, formerly the great wool market of Wales, its prices ruling over the country from Pwllheli to Llangollen.

Eight fairs were held each year according to John Williams who published his history of the town in 1830. The dates were; 8 March, 23 April, 21 June, 10 August, 17 September, 25 October, 11 December and on the second Tuesday afterwards. It is recorded that villagers from twenty miles distance brought their produce to Llanrwst market.

A busy market day in Ancaster Square

Early Days

1

The name of Llanrwst is encountered as far back as 845 AD in connection with a sanguinary battle between two rival Princes. The first conspicuous feature of early Llanrwst was its church of which nothing tangible remains but it is mentioned in the Norwich Taxation of 1254 and the Lincoln Taxation of 1291.

From the time of Crecy, Welsh soldiers figured prominently in the Edwardian Army which invaded France. They served under the banner of the Black Prince, who, as Earl of Chester, drew freely on this part of North Wales. There is a record in the *Black Prince's Registers* of 1359 of the Chamberlain of North Wales being ordered to buy green and white cloth for short coats and hats for 50 Welshmen chosen to follow the Black Prince to war. This seems the first mention of uniform.

In Llanrwst's Gwydir Chapel reposes the armoured figure of Hywel Coetmor whose son, Dafydd, 'sold his paternal property Gwydir, to Jevan ap Meredydd, ancestor to John Wynn, the historian'. It was probably this association which caused the Wynns to preserve the statue. In his memoirs, Sir John Wynn writes: 'Howell Coytmor lieth buried under a fair monument in Llanrwst Church. He was Captain of a hundred Denbighshire men, with the Black Prince, at the field of Poytiers where John, King of France, was taken.'

The armour worn by Hywel Coetmor does not confirm this. It nearly resembles a suit of the early part of the next century. Sir John may have confused Poitiers with Agincourt. The effigy in Betws-y-coed Church wears armour of the Poitiers period. A company commander would be about 30 years old in 1356 so he would be a man in his seventies at the time of Owain Glyndwr's revolt in 1400 and Hywel Coetmor was one of Glynd∑wr's most active supporters.

Sir John E Lloyd writes:

> 'When Owain Glyndwr's rebellion shook the country, the Conwy Valley was under the sway of two brothers who espoused his cause. Hywel Coetmor and Rhys Gethin, who from their eyry in Cwm Llanerch near Betws-y-Coed, so harassed the town of Llanrwst that grass grew in the market-place and the deer fed in the churchyard'.

Hywel Coetmor and his brother Robert were executors of the will of Griffith Vaughan ap Griffith ap David Goch, as were Rhys Gethin and Gruffydd Leiaf, and were living – March

1398 during Richard II's reign. Along the edge of the Llanrwst slab is cut; 'Hic Jacet Howel Coytmor ap Gruffyd Vachan ap Davyd Gam'. The Betws-y-Coed figure bears: 'Hic Jacet Howel Grufyd Coytmor ap Dafydd Goch Angus Dei Misere Me'.

The *Inventory* of the Ancient Monuments Commission (East Caerns) has two photographs of the Betws-y-Coed effigy which is stated to have armour of the third quarter of the 14th century.

The Glyndwr uprising which brought suffering to Llanrwst wrought havoc in neighbouring towns. Conwy was captured in 1401 and the towns of Flint, Rhuddlan and Hope were burnt. Hywel Coetmor and his brother Rhys Gethin (whose name is preserved at Hendre Rhys Gethin in Betws-y-coed), were familiar with the district and were therefore the more to be feared. The Abbey of Aberconwy at Maenan suffered. Buildings were destroyed but whether this was the work of Glyndwr's men or the soldiers of Henry IV is uncertain. The abbey would have been a tempting place to loot, and the Abbot favoured Glyndwr. He was denounced as a rebel in 1406. Reference to the sacking of the Abbey is encountered in the reign of Henry VI. In October 1448 the Court of Westminster issued a pardon to the Abbot for a debt of £10 following a petition, showing that the house was burnt in the time of the War of Wales, and all the books, vestments, chalices and their other ornaments spoiled (ie taken as spoil) and carried away. The monks subsequently repaired 'a great part of their house'.

The men of Llanrwst set about restoring their damaged town but they were not to enjoy a peaceful period of time. By 1450 the House of Lancaster and the House of York resorted to the sword to resolve which House should reign. Denbigh was a Yorkist stronghold; the Conwy area was Lancastrian on account of the blood relationship of leading families with the Tudors. The wooded slopes of the Vale afforded excellent hiding places. Above Gwydir rises the precipitous slope of Carreg-y-gwalch (Rock of the Falcon). Here in a cave amid the great oaks the leading Lancastrian had his headquarters.

Dafydd ap Jenkin earned the title of the Welsh Robin Hood from his custom of dressing his followers in green, obviously for camouflage, but thereby starting many legendary tales. 'He held waste the Duke of Yorke's estate in Denbighland,' wrote Sir John Wynn, 'in revenge whereof the King sent Will. Herbert,.... Earl of Pembroke in Edward IV's time, came with a great army to recover the castle of Harddlech. He also wasted with fire and sword all Nantconwy.'

Sir John quotes the Welsh rhyme (interpreted):

> 'At Harddlech and Denbigh every house was in flames,
> And Nantconwy in cinders,
> Fourteen hundred from our Lord and sixty and eight more.'

Lord Herbert 'consumed the whole burrough of Llanrwst, and all the Vale of Conwy besides, to cold coals, whereof the print is yet extant, the very stones of the ruins of manie habitations, in and along my demaynes, carrying yet the colour of fire'. The writer adds that Nantconwy was thickly wooded and all Denbigh, Caernarfon and Merioneth counties seemed one forest having few inhabitants.

The loss of manuscripts given to the flames possibly accounts for paucity of information about this period. It may be assumed that after the 1468 raid no structure in this area remained intact. Probably the church was thatched, as it had to be rebuilt. Its completion date is considered to be 1470. The establishment of the Tudor dynasty in 1485 enabled a fresh start to be made. The 'new' church built on the site of the ruined building consisted of one aisle and a chancel. Probably the nearby monastery had never properly recovered from its sacking in Glynd∑wr's uprising when this fresh trouble occurred.

The next event to disturb the town's equanimity was in 1536 when Henry VIII ordered the dissolution of the monasteries. Up to this date Llanrwst must have been under the influence of the nearby abbey. A document of 1553 alludes to 'the highway leading down from the late Monastery of Conwy to the town of Llanroost'. It had evidently been constructed by the laybrothers. The road was not continued down the valley to the north. The monks seem to have favoured the roads which climb east to Eglwysbach and Llanddoged.

Llanrwst Church now had the King for its head instead of the Pope. The dissolution affected not only the life of the church but the town's administration. As Llanrwst was not a borough with a charter it was governed (in all but the most important matters) by the Vestry. Affairs were in the hands of the incumbent, wardens and overseers of the poor and of the highways and the Constable. All parishioners were expected to take office in rotation. Service was gratuitous. The Constables were chosen in turn. They had no experience and no authority but that temporarily afforded them by virtue of their office. Their task was made easier by the simple expedient of 'hue and cry' whereby the public had to create a disturbance when any misdemeanour was noticed.

It was at this time that Cromwell made compulsory the recording in every Parish of baptisms and burials. Llanrwst's first sheepskin registers made their appearance around this time.

Only occasional references are encountered of early Tudor times but these are sufficient to indicate that buildings of consequence existed before the days of Elizabeth I. Ket's rebellion in Norfolk occurred in 1549 and Sir John's uncle, Griffith Wynn, who was in the fight, brought home Ket's horse with a velvet saddle to Gwydir. In recording this Sir John mentions that Griffith was 'born in Gwydir'. Another uncle, Robert, served in the war with France (1544) and received a shot in his leg at the capture of Boulogne. Years later when the old soldier had retired to his Conwy home, Plas Mawr, he visited Gwydir. His leg occasioned such pain that Sir John examined it and found 'a hard thing' which proved to be the French bullet. It was extracted by a surgeon.

Elsewhere Sir John mentions that he was at variance with his Uncle Owen whose men had carried hay to Cae'r Melwr across Gwydir land. The Cae'r Melwr of his day must have existed long before the dates on the present building. William Salesbury was born at Plas Isa, which indicates that the house dated from early Tudor times. These references, fragmentary though they are, establish Llanrwst's importance after the Wars of the Roses. The dimensions of Llanrwst at this period could not have been large. Sir John refers to it as 'a village'. Its design had probably differed but little when it was described in 1830 as having five streets, four lanes and a market square. A document of 1558 refers to Mathebrwd. The area stretched from Afon y Glyn to y Bryn, Melin, and 'in breadth from the said stream to the highway leading from the church of Llanrwst towards the town of Denbigh.'

Wagons and carts would be used on roads such as the one to Denbigh but for less frequented areas packhorses were favoured. Mules and donkeys were fitted with panniers and sacks of grain would be carried across a horse's back. Sir John Wynn described Caernarvonshire as 'the most rugged, barren, unpassable country in all Wales'. So serious was the surface of roads that an Act was passed prohibiting carts to be used unless they had 'broad wheels'. Denbigh was the recognised entrepôt, and stage wagons carrying goods (and sometimes impecunious passengers) plied regularly between Denbigh and London. In his *Carriers' Cosmography* of 1637, John Taylor writes:

The carriers of Denbigh in Wales do lodge at Bosom's Inn every Thursday – probably Blossoms or Bosoms Inn, St Lawrence Lane, near Cheapside where the Chester carriers lodged on a Thursday.

The journey between Llanrwst and London would be by horseback. Sir John Wynn, writing in 1612 from the White Hart Inn, reported that he had 'come safely to London after eleven days travel'. Sir John's sons when bound for school or university travelled in pairs, probably accompanied by menservants. Though the gentry and prosperous yeoman farmers could afford saddle horses, for the poor there was no other way to cross country but on foot. Even for the horseman travel was not easy. Young Richard Wynn (4th Baronet) visiting his wife's home, Chirk Castle, boasted that he had taken only three falls on the way whereas his man had sustained five or six.

After the Restoration the Wynns were able to procure a coach to enhance their dignity though the state of the roads made travel an ordeal. The 'rotten pavements' between Gwydir and Cae'r Melwr, complained Sir Richard, had shaken their coach but it still held out.

Meanwhile Lower Gwydir was being steadily enlarged. A plan included in a county map of 1720 shows the house surrounding a quadrangle and the entry has a gabled gatehouse. Reference to this gatehouse is contained in a *memorandum* made by Sir John Wynn in 1597:

To finish the pigeon house. Finish the gatehouse chamber and the maid's chamber within. 'In' the hops. Finish the causeway in Carrege dw (du).
Slate the cattle houses. Make a cellar for a burial in Llanrwst Churchyard.
Make the cellar in Havod Ryske. Make a crosshedge and ditch where I mean to make my utmost court, beyond the pigeon house. Inclose my park, except the lower side, which I mean to leave undone until my game increase. Build 4 houses in Llanrwst where Katherine Lloyd dwells and 3 others where John Cooke dwells. Repair the tanning house and lease it to a tanner. Make a dining chamber in your house in Caernarfon. And a square stair to go up to it and plaster your bed chamber and make a chimney in the chamber next to the garden and a study for yourself.

The existing ornate entrance is apparently part of the alterations effected early in the 19th century. John Wynn ap Meredith died in 1559; the date 1555 probably refers to the time he erected buildings at Gwydir.

The Elizabethans, having no counter-attractions, set store on beautifying their gardens. Families were musical and addicted to good living. From the frequent references to musical instruments it would seem that Gwydir kept an orchestra. Sir John's sons were instructed in instrumental and vocal music.

When the heir, John Wynn, went to Bedford School in 1597 he was instructed in Music in addition to learning Latin, Grammar, Greek, Hebrew, French, Italian and the precepts of Religion. His diet, board and lodging cost £13. 2. 3 a year. The boy had his own bedding and a silver spoon. Sir John in 1621 was told of a young musician who was good on the bass viol and virginals and could teach young gentlemen. William Wynn in 1623 offered to buy a 'viall de Gambo' for a kinswoman and send it by carriers. She also received a viol and a book of songs. Another of Sir John's memos is:

To send the trumpet with Wynn arms. Harken the violin and bass viol in Llandoged. Send to Cousin John Lewys for his lute; send to Chester for it and the loan of a cornet. Borrow a lute from Mostyn.

There are references to gifts of fruit or wine. Sir Richard Wynn's father-in-law offered to send Sir John Wynn nectarines and fig trees to plant at Gwydir. Humphrey Jones, Mayor of Beaumaris (whom Sir John terms 'cousin') reports when a wine ship from Gascony or a Spanish ship with oranges anchors in the roads. He also sent 'by the boatman' two hogheads of Claret to Sir John at Gloddaeth; and spices and a hundred prunes.

Silver plate was not lacking in Llanrwst's houses of quality. It was not merely a matter of ostentation; it was a practical investment, which was (literally) worth its weight in gold. The Civil War soon proved that when melted down it provided them with necessary and ready money.

A few extracts from Lady Grace Wynn's inventory at Cae'r Melwr – too lengthy to repro-duce in detail – will serve as an illustration:

"A great bowl with a cover, double gilt, a great frame with five plates on it for sweet-meats, a silver box with three dozen counters in it with the arms of England and of France, six great silver spoons with the crucifix upon the end of them that were my great-grandfather William Gurth ap Robin of Cochwillan's, a naked boy in silver with an inkhorn in one hand and a candlestick in the other, a big silver bowl that my mother Powell gave my son Sir Richard Wynn, twelve trencher plates with the Gwydir arms, eight trencher plates with the Archbishop's arms, two silver candlesticks with the eagles, four syllabub cups with spouts, a little posset cup which my Lady Wynn of Brainford gave the Receavour."

Sir John, though primarily interested in his own affairs was nonetheless public-spirited and undoubtedly provided employment for many families. In parts of the Conwy Valley old lead workings may be traced. A number of these were developed by Sir John who saw in them a source of trade abroad, particularly after the Thirty Years War had broken out. He also shipped lead to Bristol for forwarding to Spain. His son Maurice, who was with a merchant in Hamburg, endeavoured to further his father's aims, but finally Sir John con-fessed his lead works were 'a great charge and no gain' and devoured his rents. Another experiment was the extracting of lead, copper and alum from a mine on his property and during the search he discovered brimstone. By way of contrast he created a hop-yard on twelve acres of land near Llanrhychwyn which he let for twenty-one years, taking instead of rent half of the hops, packed and dried.

An original venture was his attempt to introduce Irish weavers to the area following a request from 'on Roper of Roper's Rest in Ireland', who suggested sending three hundred people to spin wool. Sir John answered: 'I will find them housing upon my lands about Llanrwst and Trefriw, being within a mile of my house; and all things necessary for them and money afore hand ......Woolle is to be had in this countrie good store and verie cheape.' He explains that he gives his support because it is a charitable deed 'for the good of the country and the services of my people'. Another sideline was an attempt to produce mineral water, most likely at Trefriw. It is amazing that this remarkable man found the time to be an antiquarian and historian.

THE SEVENTEENTH CENTURY

2

Plas Isa in an advanced state of ruin

To conceive Llanrwst in the latter Elizabethan days as a remote rural place when the gentry lived in luxury and the poor toiled at agriculture or weaving would misconstrue the situation. Over all the land the Spanish menace lay like an ominous cloud. An invasion by the powerful Spanish Fleet was daily anticipated. Gorse beacons were piled on the high places. Sir John (not yet knighted) as Deputy Lieutenant was responsible for military affairs in North Caernarvonshire. Levies for service in Ireland were mustered in Conwy. The trained bands were on the alert in case the Spanish Fleet profaned the soil. The defeat of the Spanish Armada brought only temporary relief. There are tales of Captain Will Myddleton of Denbigh (who in 1591 warned Sir Richard Grenville at the Azores of the approach of the Spanish Fleet) and Captain Thomas Prys of Plas Iolyn registering in Denbigh's inns when home from sea. It was not until pacific-minded James I came to the throne that peace was restored. John Wynn had been High Sheriff of Caernarvonshire in Armada year (1588) and again in 1603. Raising troops for Ireland was a source of frequent worry to John Wynn. 'They will venture any imprisonment rather than go for the Irish service,' he complained.

The County Muster Master, Captain John Owen, was killed near Conwy but nothing indicates that this was the work of rebellious militia men. There are numerous indications of unrest in the neighbourhood. Rioting was frequent when no Police Force existed.

In the summer of 1604 when John Wynn's term of office was nearing its close, Llanrwst experienced its worst 'affray', to use the official description, culminating in the murder of the Constable. What made this tragic happening particularly conspicuous was the social position of the perpetrators who came from the homes of local gentry. The affair was so serious that it was reported to the President of the Court of the Marches, Lord Zouche. John Wynn was placed in an embarrassing position as there were Wynns among the disturbers of the peace.

The Constable was the local smith, Hugh ap William ap Richard, who went by the nickname of Hugh y Go. Among the *Gwydir Papers* in the National Library of Wales are a number of statements taken by John Wynn as magistrate when he examined witnesses.

The accused were Thomas Wynn, Owen Wynn, Piers Salisbury, Mores, Thomas Lewis, William David and others who were indicted for the murder of the Constable. The tragedy occurred at the July Fair yet it was not until 15 August that John Wynn reported to Lord Zouche that he had apprehended three of the principle offenders and had issued writs for the arrest of the remainder. The Lord President was evidently dissatisfied as a week later he wrote to the High Sheriff of Denbighshire, John Lloyd of Vaynol, saying that the persons who were committed to Ruthin Gaol for complicity in the murder 'notwithstanding the heinousness of that barbarous act were suffered to go from house to house at their pleasure'. He required that they were removed to 'a straighter prison'. The case was heard in Denbigh (the county town) in September.

From various sources it is able to reconstruct the eventful day. John Wynn in his preliminary examination of the prisoners – they were conducted in the Justice Room at Gwydir – was assisted by two other local magistrates, Cadwaladr Wynn, a kinsman and Henry ap Ieuan Lloyd.

Sir John asserts that he came to the place where the murder was committed on hearing the hue and cry. He added that 'divers dear friends have laboured with the writer to spare the lives of the offenders, to whom the Sheriff and most of the country gentlemen were akin'. He claims that it was by his means that three of the offenders were arrested and sent to gaol.

John Wynn wrote to Sir Richard Lewkenor, one of the Justices of Chester, that the Constable was murdered in his own house by a company of 'swagryne gent', after striving to keep the peace. According to one witness there was disorder and quarrelling all day. Among those present at the fray were Robert and William Holland. Thomas Wynn who struck the fatal blow bore the murdered man a grudge.

The disturbances in Llanrwst were brought to a head when the 'swaggering gentlemen' endeavoured to catch a certain John ap Rice Lloyd who ran to the Constable's house for safety. But he was chased and his persecutors, finding the stout front door barred against them, went round to the rear and entering, rushed up the stairs. In an upper room several men were drinking. The fugitive dashed in and the Constable bolted the door and called upon the assailants in the King's name to keep the peace. But Lewis with his shoulder and Thomas Wynn with his foot forced the door and burst in with drawn weapons. Thomas Wynn thrust his sword into the throat of the Constable who called out, 'The villain hath kylled me', and he fell.

The murderers stabbed their weapons into bedding, searching for John ap Rice who escaped. A witness standing on Bryn y Boten saw him come through the window with Thomas

Wynn, Salisbury and Lewis after him. They failed to catch him but encountered Owen Wynn who fell down, 'and in his fall dyd hurt hymm self with his own dagger'.

Three men were duly sent to the Assizes. The relevant documents cease abruptly so the result of the trial is not recorded.

By this time John Wynn was recognised as one of the prominent men not merely of the immediate area of his home but in North Wales. Born in 1554 and educated at University and Inns of Court he was a Member of Parliament for Caernarvonshire in 1586-7 and was High Sheriff for the county the following year. On 14 May 1606 he received a knighthood, followed, on 29 June 1611, by a Baronetcy. Llanrwst benefited by his rise to fame.

An outstanding date of this period was 1610 when Sir John Wynn, having obtained the rectorial tithes of Eglwys-bach, bestowed on Llanrwst what he termed 'Jesus Hospital', a title which comprised a strange but useful amalgamation of the almshouse near the church, a free school and a weekly 'lecture', probably in the form of a religious dissertation. The 'almshouse' (singular) originally provided for eleven aged men and an old woman bedmaker, but later with the name changed to 'almshouses', cared for six old men. The school at that time was on the outskirts of the village and a stipulation was that scholars from Llanrwst, Eglwysbach and Dolwyddelan could always attend free of charge. Another clause was that the master of the school and the usher (second master) must be graduates; another that the usher would read prayers to the scholars and the inmates of the almshouses each day. For this a fee was paid. A copy of Sir John's will is in the *Calendar of Wynn Papers*. He evidently had no high regard for the encumbent for he wrote: 'I give the vicar just a cow.'

Sir John's eldest son, also Sir John, High Sheriff of Merioneth in 1611, married the daughter of Sir Thomas Cave. The marriage was not a success and Sir John travelled on the continent, dying at Lucca in 1614.

The hope of Gwydir now rested on the second son, Richard, for whom his father procured a knighthood in 1616. Educated at Lincoln's Inn he entered the Lord Chamberlain's service and subsequently became a Groom of the Bedchamber to Charles, Prince of Wales, and accompanied him and the Duke of Buckingham on their fatuous incognito mission to Spain.

In 1625, following King Charles's marriage, he was appointed treasurer to Queen Henrietta Maria and made Groom of the Bedchamber to the King and Queen. He made his home at Brentford where his wife's people lived and Gwydir saw little of the man who was to succeed Sir John. The task of managing the family home was relegated to Owen Wynn who had married Archbishop William's niece. Sir Richard loyally kept in touch with Gwydir.

Numerous messengers arrived with letters and gifts from the capital. Probably the most amazing was the arrival in 1610 of a messenger bearing King James's sword. The King had often worn it, wrote Sir Richard, but had given it to a courtier who had bestowed it on Richard. 'The blade is as good as any worn by any man in England and worth making much of.' No more is heard of this rare relic; it was probably plundered when Gwydir was sacked. On 1 March 1626 Lady Sydney wrote begging her son to hasten home, as his father was very ill and not likely to recover. Sir John, aged 75, died that day.

A new era started in the annals of Gwydir and of Llanrwst.

PLAS ISA AND SALESBURY

Plas Isa (as the name was spelt), once a landmark, is now a name without a place. The tithe map of 1844 shows its buildings in an isolated spot east of Station Road to which Plas Isa is connected by a straight lane. Sir John Wynn describes the house as 'near Llanrwst'. A younger son of the great house of Lleweni, Robert Salusbury, came to Llanrwst for his bride and married Gwenhwyfar, daughter and heiress of Rhys ab Einion Fychan of Plas Isa, Llanrwst. Their son Foulk, doubtless named after his uncle the Dean of St Asaph, married Ann, daughter of William ap Gruffydd ap Robin of Cochwillan. They had two sons, Robert and William. Robert succeeded to the estate but his younger brother, William, the scholar who translated the New Testament into Welsh, attained the greater fame.

Robert left no heir but his two heiresses established links with Gwydir. Gwen, the elder, married Griffith Wynn of Berth Ddu and Elin, the younger, Owen Wynn of Cae'r Melwr, doubtless bringing these two properties as dowry. Robert's wife was Lowry, sister of Dr Ellis Price (Dr Coch) of Plas Iolyn and William married her sister, Catherine. On the death of Robert (his will is dated 1540) William inherited Plas Isa. *Publisher's note*: this would seem to confirm that W.S. was not born at Plas Isa, (see p.12). He was probably born at Cae Du, see below.

According to tradition he worked secretly on the translation of the New Testament in a small house, Cae Du, near Llansannan during the reign of the Catholic Queen. Mary died in 1558 but this great work was not published until 1567, which implies that much of it was done at Plas Isa. Wiliam's son and heir, John, of Plas Isa, according to a pedigree, married 'Mary Salusbury of Stow, Kent'.

In the University College of North Wales are several documents which, while throwing valuable light on the Salusburys of this period, do not confirm this marriage. These may introduce yet another Robert Salusbury. The first is dated 19 April 1621 and concerns an after-marriage agreement, the first parties being Robert Salusbury 'of Llanroost, Esq' and John, his son and heir, who married Jane, daughter of Mrs Mary Salusbury, widow living in Betws-yn-Rhos. Parties of the second part were Mrs Mary Salusbury, William Wynn of Llanfair, Esq and Thomas Salusbury of Alltvayan, gent; also Foulk Salusbury, the elder, of Denbigh, a linen draper. The numerous Salusbury names suggest a marriage of cousins.

The Bodysgallen Roll records the death of Robert Salusbury on 18 January 1621. John inherited Plas Isa and other property. Robert was obviously a man of consequence as in 1619 he was recommended by Sir John Wynn to be a fit person to serve on the Commission of the Peace. He is described as 'Robert Salusbury of Plas Isa, a discreet gentleman and heir of an ancient house, with land to the value of £200 a year'. The roll also enters the name of 'Mary Salusbury of Bettws yn Rhos, widowe' on 24 February 1626.

John Salusbury lived through the Civil War. He might be the John Salusbury who, with William Wynn, was responsible for collecting the Llanrwst mise. In February 1645, Colonel William Salusbury, royalist Governor of Denbigh, ordered the collectors to levy a sum sufficient to maintain three hundred men in his garrison and a troop of horses.

Llanrwst Register records the baptism of Dorothy, daughter of John Salusbury of Plas Isa, on 12 July 1664. Hugh Salusbury was baptised on 29 September 1638. The burial of John Salusbury of Plas Isa, armiger, is entered on 28 December 1662.

The next document in the *Maenan Collection* is dated 1 April 1664 and concerns the before-marriage settlements of John Salusbury, gent, to Jane Foulkes, one of the daughters of Humphrey Foulkes of Ereithlyn. The marriage is entered in the Eglwys-bach Church Register. By the settlement Plas Isa and other property was settled on John's son and heir, Thomas Salusbury. Thomas Salusbury lived until 1667 but was in debt, possibly on account of the war. On 20 June 1664 he leased Plas Isa for 99 years to John Griffith of Llanddyfnan, Anglesey, on trust that he, Thomas, should receive all rents and profits for his lifetime.

In his will of 5 June 1667, Thomas makes his wife Jane sole executrix. Thomas's two brothers were William and John, the former described as 'clerk'. William was empowered to dispose of lands to pay his brother's debts and also to pay a yearly payment of £70 to his brother's wife. William appears to have retired to Llangernyw, but retained the designation of William Salusbury of Plas Isa according to Llanrwst Register, which enters the baptism of two of his children born in Llangernyw. Llanrwst Register records the baptisms of Robert Salusbury of Plas Isa, 8 November 1670 in Llangernyw Church and John, son of William Salusbury of Plas Isa, 1672 also in Llangernyw Church. William Salusbury of Plas Isa was buried on 23 December 1672 according to the Llanrwst Register. (i.e. the same day that his son was baptised, see below). It would appear from the original will of Margaret Salusbury of Plas Isa, that she was William's widow. The will was dated 6 October 1690 with a codicil added in 1699. She appointed her son John (? William's brother) as her sole executor, leaving him a close called 'Keven y Ddol'. There is an entry in the Llanrwst Register of the burial on 11 January 1689 of a Thomas Salusbury (altered to Salesbury).

Some entries concern Salusburys who are described as 'of Llanrwst' evidently implying that they were not of the Plas Isa branch. A John Salusbury 'of Llanrwst' was buried on 10 June 1663, the year following the internment of John Salusbury, armiger, of Plas Isa. Other Salusbury entries in the register are;

> 1635 – Buried Richard, infant son of John Salusbury of Plas Isa – 31 December.
> 1667 – Buried Robert, son of Thomas Salusbury of Llanrwst – 31 December.
> 1669 – Baptised Elen, daughter of Thomas Salusbury of Llanrwst – 16 January.
> 1670 – Buried Edward Salusbury, Llanrwst – 30 October.
> 1670 – Baptised Robert Salusbury of Plas Isa in Llangernyw Church – 8 November.
> 1672 – John, son of William Salusbury of Plas Isa, baptised in Llangernyw Church 23 December.
> 1674 – John, son of John Salusbury of Caer Berllan and Anna, his wife, was baptised 2 January (?1674).

The Eglwys-bach Register records a burial of Dorothy Salusbury – 2 January.

Foulke Salusbury of Gwytherin is named in 1697.

The Wynn Papers mention a Captain Salusbury, Lieutenant in the Caernarvonshire Militia, and also state that Captain Thomas Salusbury 'had killed one Thomson of the general guard' in a duel. The Salusburys appear to have severed their connection with Plas Isa by 1734 as the vestry book alludes to 'the owners of Plas Isa' without mentioning the name. When Llwyd made his list of houses in 1699, Plas Isa belonged to Robert Salusbury, LL B, of Jesus College, Oxford.

THE BRIDGE

Llanrwst Bridge has remained the town's outstanding feature since its erection in 1636. The elegant but sturdy structure replaced an earlier one, which was decrepit after years of service and was no longer safe. Romantic tales have grown about the bridge but it was a business proposition undertaken by the quarter sessions of the two counties concerned, as the structure was part of the King's Highway. A request for a new bridge came before a jury at the General Sessions at Denbigh in 1627. It was stated that 'the public and common bridge' had for many years been 'in the greatest decay so that neither the King's subjects, nor horses, carts nor carriages, could come and go without great danger to life'.

The jury decided that Denbighshire must undertake their half share of the cost of the bridge, which was estimated at £1,000. The Wynns took a keen interest in the provision of a

The bridge in 1780 with Tu-hwnt-i'r-bont on the right hand side

new structure for the welfare of the town which coincided with the interests of the family. The bridge was a vital link in the chain connecting Gwydir with Cae'r Melwyr, Berth-ddu and other parts of the estate. Owen Wynn at home watched the leisurely developments with apprehension and in 1633 he submitted an order 'touching the decay of Llanrwst Bridge' and had the case removed to the Great Assizes. An Act of Parliament was passed approving the scheme. Caernarfon had to raise their moiety but were backward. In 1634 the Caernarvonshire Magistrates reported to the Government that they had imposed a levy of £400 and would raise the remaining £100 later, but having been reproved for their dilatoriness, they levied the £500.

The bridge has three cutwaters, which are extended to coping level where they form refuges for pedestrians. Stone panels rise over the apex of the centre arch. The south panel bears the Stuart Arms and the date 1636. A sundial was added later. The inner side of the north panel is also dated 1636. The outer face bears the Prince of Wales' feathers, now weathered. The name of Inigo Jones is persistently associated with the bridge. No written testimony supports this but there is a logical explanation. Sir Richard Wynn, Treasurer to the Queen and Groom of the Bedchamber, a conspicuous figure in court circles, would be well known to Inigo Jones, who at this time, was Surveyor General. A word from Sir Richard that he was interested in the bridge adjoining his house would have caused Inigo Jones to pay particular attention to the scheme.

The story that Inigo was a local man who had been helped by the family at Gwydir can have no foundation. Sir John Rhys who edited the 1883 version of *Pennants Tours* points out that in the mass of Gwydir papers Inigo's name is never once mentioned. Undoubtedly the design is the work of a master. The west arch collapsed in 1675. The original springers remained but the arch is of poorer workmanship. John Williams, who asserted that the bridge was designed by Inigo adds that 'two of the arches were built by a superior genius to the one who built the arch next to Gwydir.

It is unthinkable that an architect who designed a bridge which still stands up to traffic should have two magnificent arches and one faulty arch. There must be a logical explanation and it can be found in the Civil War days. It seems so obvious that it was deliberately wrecked and repaired hastily under the exigency of a campaign. This western arch gave trouble for a long time. Sometime in the 1670s Sir John Wynn, 5th Baronet, informed the Justices of the Peace that 'the work of rebuilding Llanrwst Bridge which has now fallen down must be undertaken before winter'. In 1678 the Caernarvonshire Justices were compelled to expend a further £15 on repairs to the bridge.

In the Caernarvonshire Record Office is an account of further repair work undertaken in 1702 at a cost of 'not less than £90'. It is of interest to note that the surveyor in his report emphasised that the empty places were to be made up with good building stone and lime 'instead of earth, sand and other rubbish'. The portion under repair was described as being 'ruinous and in great decay'.

WAR IMPENDING

Llanrwst Bridge had lost none of its pristine beauty when the clouds of war gathered. They were, it is true, no nearer Wales than the Scottish border. Here the Presbyterian Scots were mustering to resist by force if necessary the attempt to impose on them the religion of the Church of England. In 1639 the trained bands of England and Wales were called out to meet the situation. Owen Wynn was captain in the Llanrwst Company. It was an underwritten law that in an emergency such as this the gentry should set an example of service. Owen was a Deputy Lieutenant and therefore responsible for the organisation of military matters in his area but he seems to have lacked military enthusiasm. The Lord President of the Council of Wales (? the Earl of Bridgwater) had occasion to reprimand him.

The President had issued instructions for enrolling all men between sixteen and sixty according to the ancient militia practice. The men of Llanrwst resented and riots followed. Two men escaped from prison and were to be seen 'swaggering securely from one alehouse to another'. In October that year Colonel Thomas Wynn of Glynllifon wrote reproving Owen Wynn for not attending the general muster at Caernarfon, especially as his troops were badly armed.

The Scottish expedition proved farcical and the following year more levies were called out for a second attempt. Denbighshire contributed three hundred men and Caernarvonshire one hundred and sixty. The next year horse and foot were transported to Ireland, the new trouble centre. There is no indication that Llanrwst men were involved.

Sir Richard Wynn, Squire of Gwydir and MP for Liverpool, through his London contacts was quick to realise the inevitability of war between King and Parliament and expressed his fears to his brother Maurice who was then in London. The latter wrote home to Owen that Sir Richard (who lived on the outskirts of Brentford) had proved himself 'with powder, muskets, pikes, headpieces, swords and bows and arrows to defend himself if the times prove bad'.

Llanrwst Bridge built in 1636

It would seem that these were intended for Gwydir, as Maurice comments that he did not know how many horseloads they would make as the arms had not been packed. There is an ambiguous observation in a draft letter from Sir Richard to his 'Lieutenant- Colonel' having thrown up his command. This appears to be the only suggestion that Sir Richard might have held a commission. Sir Richard considered events so serious that he drew up his will. Colonel Hugh Wynn at Bodysgallen raised a regiment of foot at his own expense. Though only twenty-two years of age he led them to join the Chester Garrison.

Apart from a mild panic in the area when a rumour was spread that Irish Catholics were plotting to seize Conwy, nothing of consequence disturbed the peace of Llanrwst until the autumn of 1645. The King, following his defeat at Rowton Moor on 24 September, fled to Denbigh Castle, and after a few days rest, made his way back through Ruthin and Chirk to England. He left instructions for Sir William Vaughan, who commanded the horse, to raise men from the border garrisons to relieve Lord Byron who was surrounded in Chester. Vaughan's force was surprised on Denbigh Green by Parliamentarians from Chester and were defeated. The Royalist foot took refuge in the castle. Sir William Vaughan with most of the horses headed for Llanrwst. Owen Wynn describes their arrival:

'Sir William Vaughan, having been defeated near Denbigh that day, fled with the remainder of his horses, in number about nine hundred, towards the mountains and that night fell upon the house of Sir Richard Wynn, where they stayed five days and on going, rifled the house, Sir Richard being absent in Parliament.'

With the Royalist horse was Trooper Richard Symonds who entered in his diary: 'Sir Richard Wynn lives at Guydur, a fair seate in the Parish of Llanrust yet in Caernarvonshire.' His comment does not coincide with Owen Wynn's account. Symonds writes: 'the horse got to Llanrwst that night, twelve miles distant; next morning dispersed to quarters.' It was obvious that Gwydir could not house nine hundred. By 4 November it was safe for the Royalist Infantry to venture to leave Denbigh and Symonds entered in his diary, 'came our foot to us out of the castle to Llanrwst'.

After the surrender of Chester on 3 February, the Roundheads turned their attention to the invasion of North Wales. Ruthin and Denbigh were first and while the sieges were in progress the Commander-in-Chief, Major-General Thomas Mytton, with an advance party explored the way to Llanrwst bridgehead, preparatory to advancing against Caernarfon Castle which Byron had made his headquarters. It was in March 1646 that General Mytton made his first appearance in Llanrwst. Maurice Wynn, a bachelor, had taken charge of Gwydir, which had been rendered unfit for Owen Wynn to dwell in after it had been sacked and pillaged. Here Mytton stayed during his inspection of the terrain and on departing he issued to Maurice Wynn a certificate testifying to his 'cheerful entertainment'.

Following the surrender of Ruthin in April, Mytton again arrived at Llanrwst. These two visits suggest that the bridge had been damaged sufficiently to interfere with his plans – in fact Byron had suggested to Sir John Owen, the Royalist Governor of Conwy, that Llanrwst Bridge should be rendered unserviceable. Horse and foot could have forded the river but the breaking down of the western section would prevent the passage of the heavy guns required for battering the stout walls of Caernarfon and Conwy. The rubbish found in the damaged arch suggests a hurried wartime repair and undoubtedly siege guns were used against these two strongholds.

On this occasion Mytton was the guest of Owen and Grace Wynn at Cae'r Melwr. On his departure the General issued a 'protection' to Owen. A document now in the National

Library of Wales informed the Parliamentary forces under Mytton's command that 'on pain of death' they were to respect the family property and possessions of the holder. (see p. 26)

It was not until Richard married in 1654 that the family returned to Gwydir and Sir Owen, contrary to all expectations, seems content at the removal. These courtesies extended by the Wynns to the King's enemies doubtless enraged Sir John Owen who despatched troopers to drive off two hundred of Owen Wynn's cattle. This would still further embitter the Wynns who were already prejudiced by the treatment accorded them by Vaughan's cavalry.

When Aberystwyth surrendered to the Parliament, Colonel Roger Whitley, the Royalist Governor, marched a hundred survivors by way of Harlech to Llanrwst Bridge on the way to Denbigh to continue the struggle. After Caernarfon was surrendered in June, Mytton turned his attention to Conwy and on 9 August, by a night attack, obtained possession of the town, though the castle held out until 18 November. Sir John Owen's only son Richard was one of the defenders of Flint Castle to judge by a letter written by Major David Pennant to Owen Wynn in which he referred to warrants of contributions 'due to Captain Wynn when he served in Flint Castle'. The first Civil War ended with the fall of Harlech in March 1647. The peace, which followed, was ephemeral.

In March 1648, Colonel Poyer, Parliamentary Governor of Pembroke Castle declared for the captive King and smouldering revolt flared up in many parts of the country. Charles, exiled Prince of Wales, sent Lord Byron to North Wales and the border counties with a commission to enlist Royalists. Having failed to gather any considerable force in Delamere Forest where he was joined by Colonel Richard Whitley, Byron moved towards Shrewsbury while Whitley rode to Llanrwst Bridge where a party of Cavaliers from Anglesey waited for him to join forces with the islanders. Mytton was ordered to suppress the revolt in Anglesey. At the head of some one thousand five hundred horse and foot he marched by way of Wrexham. Malbon, the Nantwich diarist, records the route, which was by way of Denbigh and St Asaph. At Abergele, Mytton turned and marched to Llanrwst Bridge in preference to using Conwy Ferry.

The Parliamentary victory at Beaumaris revived the hopes of a permanent peace. Sir Richard Wynn did not long survive the execution of King Charles. He died in his home at Brainford (as Brentford was called) and was buried on 18 July 1649 in Wimbledon Church. Sir Richard's sole executor, his brother Maurice, informed Sir Owen that Sir Richard had left a silver medallion bearing the heads of King Charles I and his Queen to be kept at Gwydir as a memento that he 'had been a servant to both'.

Sir Owen and Lady Grace remained at Cae'r Melwr until their son, Sir Richard, in 1654, married Sarah, the attractive daughter of Sir Thomas Myddleton of Chirk Castle. Sarah's face still smiles from one of the brasses in Gwydir Chapel. It was a love match. Richard and his bride made Cae'r Melwr their home and Sir Owen and Lady Grace returned to Gwydir. Owen was a man of ability and his father considered him the most fitted to manage the Gwydir estate. He was educated at Westminster School, Eton and Cambridge University and also trained in the household of the Bishop Lincoln.

Sir Owen Wynn appears to have balanced adroitly on the political fence. When Sheriff of Caernarvonshire in 1652 he proclaimed Cromwell as Protector. Three years later he held the same office in Denbighshire. It was an anomalous position as this was the year when as a man of Royalist sympathies he was threatened with sequestration. When summoned before the Commissioners for Sequestration who met at Conwy he wrote informing them that he never had been of the King's Party, neither had he taken up arms for the King. His estate had never been sequestered nor compounded for. He had never been disobedient to the Parliamentary Government 'but suffered much from plundering at their hands'. He begged that he might not be ranked as a delinquent. In another statement he emphasised that his brother, the late Sir Richard, never attended the King's 'Parliament' at Oxford. Sir Owen pointed out that he had never acted as a Commissioner of Array for the King. He sent a copy of his justification to John Bradshaw, Chief Justice of Chester, adding that he had been sick and was unfit to travel and was sixty-four years of age. He asked for the Judges' advice. It would appear that Sir Owen was not penalised.

In the summer of 1659 the peace again was disturbed by the uprising in Cheshire of Royalists and Presbyterians. The aged Sir Thomas Myddleton, erstwhile Major General for Parliament, brandished his sword in Wrexham market place and declared for King Charles II. It may be assumed that his dashing son-in-law, Richard Wynn, was at his side. When the rising was easily crushed in August, Sir Thomas escaped and Richard, who had lost his horse in the fighting, took refuge in the Llanrwst district. In September John Evans the trumpeter and another trooper arrived searching for him to demand his submission. As a result Richard, though he had been Sheriff of Caernarvonshire the previous year, found himself a prisoner in Caernarfon Castle. His mother, Lady Grace, by a handsome bribe, prevailed upon the Governor Colonel Thomas Madryn, to issue a pass permitting Richards 'to proceed to his house at Caermelwr for the space of twenty eight days'. He was then allowed out on parole.

The following year Charles II rode triumphantly into his capital. Richard in London witnessed the Monarch's return. The turn of events was opportune for Sir Owen was sinking fast.

APPENDIX

Major-General Thos. Mytton's Protection

To all and singular Com(m)anders Captaines Officers and Souldiers whatsoever under my command or otherwise imployed in ye Kg and Parliament's service and to all other whom these may in any wise concern.

For as much as for prevention of ye Violence and rapine of ye Souldiers ye Body, Cattles, Chattles, household stuffe apparrell Linnens, Moneys Plate, jewels, horses, Goods and other ye p(er)sonal estat whatsoever of or belonging to this Bearer Owen Wynne of Caermelwr in ye County of Denbigh Esq are desired to receive p(ro)tection from mee (whoses name is subscribed) being ye Commander in Chief appointed by Parliament of all ye Parliaments forces within ye six Countyes of North Wales; These now therefore to charge and com(m)and you every one of you upon sight hereof to forebeare to seize, take, carry away, plunder or otherwise in any sort to intermedle with ye aforesaid Body, Goods cattles or other ye said p(er)sonable Estate whatsoever without order or warrant either under my hand, or under ye hands of ye Com(m)ittee appoynted by Parliament for North Wales first had and obtained upon payne of death to be inflicted on you by ye Court of Martial Law if you offend herein by disobeying this my p(ro)tection. Given under my hand at my Quarters in Guedir in ye County of Caernarfon on the 25th day of April annodomini 1646.

THE RESTORATION

When the interrupted entries in the Llanrwst Church Register were resumed at the Restoration the first recorded burial was on 13 April when Sir Owen Wynn, 3rd Baronet, was interred at the age of sixty-eight. It was appropriate that he should be the first as it marked the end of an era. What had happened to the register during the eighteen years, which followed the outbreak of war, is not known. No entry occurs between1642 and 1660. Pages do not appear to have been ripped out; possibly the register was concealed. When Sir Owen's son Richard succeeded he was about thirty-five years old. Parliament was dissolved in November and Sir Richard was elected for the next parliament the following year and served as Shire Member until his death. The coming of peace saw Colonel Hugh Wynne of Bodysgallen, his fighting days ended, back at the family house, Berth Ddu where he continued to serve as Deputy Lieutenant and JP.

Sir Richard was also a magistrate and participated in the Government of Denbigh. His only daughter, Mary, was born in 1661. A son John, born in October 1667, only lived until the following January. Sir Richard spent much time in London and seems to have been extravagant. He stayed for a time in the King's Head Tavern, Fleet Street. There was still unrest in the land and orders were issued for arming the militia. Among the undertakings of the Denbighshire sessions in 1662 was the repair of the ancient bridge over the River Machno called Pont-rhyd-gynon on the road from Llanrwst to Penmachno. The *Wynne Papers* contain homely touches such as the recovery of Sir Richard and family from the measles and Thomas Bulkely sending Sir Richard a present of four hundred oysters, 'a great novelty'.

Sir Richard, having inherited the baronetcy, removed to Gwydir as the demesne house. Lady Grace went to Cae'r Melwr, which became the dower house and she remained there for many years. The ornamental coat-of-arms over the mantel of the largest front upper room bears the date 1663 and the initials G. W. The stables have a heavy door frame on the lintel of which is cut R. W. 1658, for Sir Richard when Caermelwr was his home before his father died. A letter from Maurice Wynn to Lady Grace announces: 'the small-pox is in two places in Llanrwst' in 1664. 'Two grandchildren of Mistress Vaughan of Glanllyn are dead of it.' Sir Richard's daughter evidently referred to herself as Mally for her mother, writing to Sir Richard at the King's Head tavern, informs him that many were ill with the small-pox and that their daughter, Mally, prays for him daily.

It was customary for the usher of the Free School to read aloud news items received from London and letters sent to Gwydir must have contained dramatic information – the second Dutch war with the burning of HMS *London*, the plague of 1665 and the Fire of London, the following year. From home Colonel Hugh Wynn writes to tell Sir Richard in London that 'My lady is well and Mistress Mary Wynn very merry and full of play'. About this time the church registers are showing that the long Wynn regime was nearing its end. Burial entries record:

    1670 Maurice Wynn of Gwydir, 30 September
    1671 Lady Sara, wife of Sir Richard Wynn, 23 June
    1674 Sir Richard Wynn, bart, 4 November
    1674 Colonel Hugh Wynn of Berth Ddu, 16 December

A year before he died Sir Richard caused a small private chapel to be built at Gwydir Uchaf. It has a fine contemporary painted ceiling. The roof has its original tiles. Lady Grace Wynn gave silver plate to the chapel in 1676. There is a small gallery. The only door is a round-headed one on the northside. Above it is a shield with SRWB 1673. This is repeated on a massive beam. The small but artistic building is now under CADW. A detailed description with photographs appears in the Inventory of the Ancient Monuments Commission, East Caernarvonshire.

The only daughter of Sir Richard and Lady Sarah Wynn, Mary, was married in Westminster Abbey in 1678 to Robert Bertie, Lord Willoughby de Eresby, later Marquis of Lindsey and Duke of Ancaster. Gwydir remained in the family until 1895. Shortly after his marriage Lord Willoughby was elected Common Burgess of Denbigh, thereby gaining a Parliamentary vote. With him were sworn burgesses 'John Ffarthing a gentleman attending the said Lord' and 'Morris Jones of Llanrwst, clre, vsher of ye school'.

In 1661, possibly in celebration of the birth of Mary Wynn, Maurice Wynn, her bachelor uncle, caused a town hall to be erected in Bryn y Boten market place. William describes it as a plain substantial structure. Mr W Bezant Lowe states that the building was burnt down and another was built by Lord Willoughby early in 1800. It is this connection that gives Ancaster Square its name. 'An adjournment of the general quarter sessions were wont to be held in this hall.' writes John Williams in 1830, 'and old persons now living recollect the steps from the square.'

Lewis, after stating that the town hall was erected at the expense of Maurice Wynn Esq of Cae'r Melwr, adds that the arms of the Wynns were displayed over the door and with them the initials of the founder with the date 1661. These stones have been preserved. Over these was a clock with a cupola containing the market-bell surmounted by a large gilt eagle. In 1964 the town hall was demolished to make room for a parking place.

The severance of a long connection with the Gwydir family and Llanrwst almost coincides with the end of the Stuart Dynasty. If there appears to be a tendency to glamorise the Gwydir association with the town it is because there is such a wealth of material available and it makes good reading. Yet there is no inexorable division between rich and poor. Sir Richard Wynn, baronet, caught measles as effectively as a cottager in a cegin.

A tribute to the busy housewives whose knitting needles supplied stockings for the Llanrwst Market is paid by Robert Wynn who wrote from college asking for Llanrwst stockings to be sent to him as the dye from the hosiery sold in the university city ran and stained his skin.

The emphasis is on Gwydir not because the Wynns were affluent but because they left records. No tanner or glover set down in writing the 'short and simple annals of the poor'. Trade and housework must have been carried on much as it is today though with more 'do-it-yourself' and less push-button luxury! There were lazy, untidy men as the state of the churchyard testified; there were men who worked for the love of knowledge like Sir Owen Wynn who was interested in alchemy, chemistry and metallurgy.

THE PARISH CHURCH

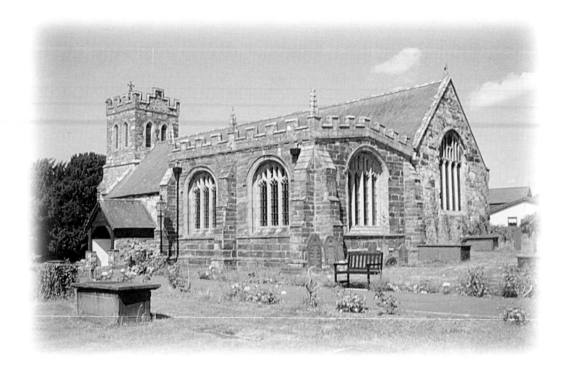

3

St Grwst's Church

The present church was completed about the year 1470 to replace the medieval building destroyed by the Yorkists. It possessed, according to an old account, one aisle and a gallery. There may have been portions of an earlier building as Edward Lhwyd c. 1699 alludes to 'a chappel yt stood formerly where y lowest part of y church is now'.

The most conspicuous feature of the church is its rood screen, which is exquisitely carved and an object of rare beauty. It is ponderous for a building of this size and there are indications that it has been shaped to fit into place. Archdeacon D T Thomas considered that it was made for the church when it was rebuilt in 1470 adding 'we may conclude that the rood-loft was then set up and that its artificers were the skilled lay-brothers of Maenan Abbey!' This requires analysing. It might well represent the handiwork of monastic craftsmen, but it is more likely to have been devised at that period for the abbey, which also suffered despoliation and damage during the wars. It is known that the abbey was taken down on order from Henry VIII who wanted the material for restoring Caernarfon Castle. John Wynn ap Meredith was the Royal Steward for the abbey at this time and he would probably order the screen to be removed to the nearest church. Moreover, it would be hard to imagine the most boorish labourer wantonly wrecking an object of such beauty during demolition work. If not 'religious' he would have been superstitious. The screen appears to have been re-erected back to front so that the sockets for the rood and its images faced the altar and could not be seen by the congregation. When the Duke of Beaufort on his 'progress' as Lord President of Wales and the Marches stopped at Gwydir in 1684, his secretary, Thomas Dineley, visited the church and entered in his journal: 'Over the Timber Arch of the Chancel near the Rood Loft lieth the ancient figure of the Crucifixion as big as life' and commenting, 'this I suppose is shown to none but the curious and rarely then'.

Formerly the loft was used as a minstrel gallery. When the last Baronet of Hawarden, the Rev Sir Stephen Glynne, visited Llanrwst in 1847 during his inspection of ancient churches, he described Llanrwst as:

'a poor parish church having a nave and chancel undivided...... At the west side is a modern tower, low and pseudo-Gothic; the south porch also is modern......the only feature worthy of much notice is the roodloft, which is in a very perfect state and of much beauty.......the screen exhibits ten arched compartments on each side of the holy doors.'

The structure was in good repair when the Rural Dean made his report in 1729 though he found the flagging uneven. He commented: 'the pulpit and cushion are worm-eaten. The pews and benches are ruinous. The church-yard is not kept clean.'

A period when the church suffered from neglect followed and the report of the Rural Dean in 1749 shows considerable deterioration.

'The few seats are irregular and bad, the Reading Seat, pulpit and altar rails I find most covered with the droppings of birds. The communion table and rails are loose in the joynts, rotten and ready to fall to pieces'.

Plate consisted of a large silver chalice, gilt, the gift of Lady Grace Wynn, also 'one of plain silver, old and dinged'. A tower was added to the church at the expense of the Rev H Holland Edwards, when rector early in the nineteenth century. In 1687 Bishop Barrow united the rectory and vicarage and in future the incumbent was known as the rector.

The earliest features of the structure are a triple lancet window on the north side and a small round-headed doorway on the south. The west window is perpendicular. The church fabric was renovated in 1852. A north aisle was added in 1884 by Archbishop Hugh Jones, when the east end was screened off for an organ chamber and vestry. At this time the western gallery and pews were removed. The tower arch was opened out and the basement screened off. The pulpit with its panel of screen work was placed at the south-east angle of the nave, seats installed for the choir and the sacrarium raised three steps. The font is of early design but is on a modern plinth. In a document of 1735 is an allusion to 'a wooden image of saint in ye brod-loft'. An unusual carved head preserved may be an unflattering portrait of St Grwst.

'The church contains several reliques of antiquity,' wrote John Williams in 1830, 'the music gallery, the pulpit and the reading desk were brought here from the Abbey of Conwy at Maenan when the monastery was dissolved.'

The old rectory was described in 1791 as 'a dwelling house, a barn and a stable, having seven small bays all under one roof, covered with straw'. In 1832 an excellent house was erected at a cost of one thousand six hundred pounds, but it had no glebe except the garden and about three-quarters of an acre of mountain enclosure. The present rectory is on the

Above: The former St Mary's Church
Below: The Churchgates and almshouses on the left

Llanddoged road and the former known as Glan-y-borth was used as the town hall and council chamber. For several years now, it has been a nursing home. The Church House was built in memory of Archdeacon Hugh Jones who was rector from 1868 to 1897 when Cannon John Morgan succeeded him. It cost one thousand four hundred pounds and was opened on 10 December 1899.

THE GWYDIR CHAPEL

The most unusual feature of Llanrwst Church is the Gwydir Chapel added in 1633 by Sir Richard Wynn, 2nd Baronet. The name Inigo Jones is associated with its design and possibly with some justification for it savours more of a city structure than an addition to a rural place of worship. Its incongruity struck E Hyde Hall in 1810 for he comments: 'the external appearance of the chapel is handsome, but its darker coloured stone with turrets and pinnacles does not harmonise with the white-washed parish church to which it is tied.'

Though the name of Sir Richard is, quite correctly, connected with the building of the Gwydir Chapel, it is apparent that in erecting it he was carrying out the wishes of his father, Sir John, who left one thousand pounds towards the cost. As far back as 1616 Sir John made a *memo*: 'Get a licence drawn by Steel, for the erection of a chapel in Llanrwst churchyard and have it confirmed by the Bishop.'

Three years before this Sir John was notified that the tomb he had ordered was carefully shipped from the haven of London in the *Hopewell* to be landed at Beaumaris. The tomb was packed in three chests with three or four loose stones for the wall.

In 1634 Sir Richard had a portal constructed in the west wall of the chapel so that the family and retainers could enter without passing up the ailse. Pews with quaintly carved ends – evidently the work of Gwydir craftsman – are still in position. A Latin inscription over the door and the date 1634 records Sir Richard's gift. The chapel was obviously intended for a mausoleum and it is ironical that the donor lies in Wimbledon Church. On the east wall of the chapel a marble tablet set forth in grandiloquent language the illustrious ancestry of the Wynns. The inscription begins:

'This chapel was errected Anno Dom 1633, By Sr Richard Wynn of Gwder, in the Covnty of Carnarvon, Knight & Baronet, treasurer to the high and mightie Princess Henriette Marie, Queen of England, daughter of Henry IV, King of France and wife of our sovaraigne King Charles........'

A ponderous pedigree traces the Wynns to Owen Gwynedd, Prince of Wales. There follows the family of Sir John Wynn and Sydney, his wife. There children were:

'Sir John Wynn, who died at Lvsa, in Italy; Sir Richard now living; Thomas Wynn who lyeth here; William Wynn, now living; Maurice Wynn, now living; Ellis Wynn, now lyeth buried at Whitford, in the County of Flynt; Henry Wynn, now lyving; Roger Wynn, who lyeth here; and two daughters, Mary, now lyving, married to Sr Roger Mostyn, in the County of Flynt, Knight; and Elizabeth, now lyving, married to Sr John Bodvill in the County of Carnarvon, Knight'.

'On the south side,' runs an old account, 'are two stately pyramidal columns of variegated marble, decorated with martial insignia, one to the memory of Meredith Wynn (ob 1525), the other to Sir John Wynn and Sydney, his wife.' The Latin inscriptions are on black marble.

The private chapel at Upper Gwydir (Gwydir Uchaf)

Between the columns is a tablet to John Wynn ap Meredith who died in 1559.

On the wall, now behind glass, are brass portraits, which Pennant discovered 'trampled under feet'. They represent Sir John Wynn ; Lady Sydney Wynn, his wife; Sir Owen Wynn, 3rd Baronet; Mary Wynn, wife of Sir Roger Mostyn; Lady Sarah Wynn and Kathleen Lewis, daughter of Samuel Lewis of Ffestiniog who died at the age of sixteen. The most appealing portrait is that of Sara, wife of the 4th Baronet. 'By far the most beautiful piece of engraving I ever saw,' is Pennant's tribute. It was engraved by William Vaughan and the remaining five are by Sylvanus Crue. The two Sir Richards are missing which suggests that there were other brasses which have been lost.

A large flag of freestone records in Latin the deaths of five sons. Sir John, the eldest died in Lucca in 1613, aged thirty. The others are Robert, MA and Thomas, Roger and Roger who died young.

The sad effigy of a baby in swaddling clothes perpetuates the grief of Owen Wynn and his wife, Grace, when their daughter, Sydney, born 6 September died on 8 October 1639. The alabaster is disfigured by sacrilegious knives. Sir Owen's portrait is of unusual interest because of correspondence which has survived. The London firm of engravers wrote to Maurice Wynn for instructions. Was his brother to be 'engraven'd with a face new-trimmed' or (as the writer remembered him) with a busy beard 'which he wore carelessly'. Work on the head and the face had begun but the beard would not be touched until these details were received. The engraving cost five pounds and the brass two pounds sixteen shillings.

Beside the effigy of Hywel Coetmor rests the stone coffin of Llewelyn the Great who, on his death in 1240, was buried before the altar of the abbey in Conwy. When the monastery was removed to Maenan the monks bore with them the remains of their bountiful benefactor. At the Dissolution the sarcophagus was again removed, this time to the nearest place of worship, probably on the instructions of the steward, John Wynn ap Meredith, where according to Lewis it remained 'obscured by rubbish'. In 1684 when Thomas Dudley saw the coffin he was told that the quatrefoil adornments on the side once held 'Arms of brass gilt and enamel'd' but these had been taken away by the late rebels. The Rural Dean in 1729 comments 'he was brought here by some of the Ancestors of Gwydir because they were descended from him'.

Nothing else seems to have suffered from parliamentary hands. Probably General Mytton's protection for Owen Wynn's property 'on pain of death' was still effective until the Restoration.

The church contains a number of epitaphs of interest. Perhaps the most unusual is that of the Rev Griffith Lloyd who appears to have composed his own which reads: 'Here lies the body of Griffith Lloyd of Brynniog, once the underserving schoolmaster of Llanrwst later the most undeserving Rector of Llanddoget. Buried on 15 May AD 1709. Do not say, write or think anything evil of the dead.'

A Rural Dean's epitaph reads:-

'Underneath lieth the body of Thomas Wynn AM, late Rector of this Parish and Prebendary of the Church of St Asaph who died universally lamented on the 13 July and was interred on the 16 of the same in the Year of our Lord, 1741.'

The generous rector, the Rev H Howell Holland-Edwards of Pennant, who gave the tower and did much to make possible the church of St Mary, died childless, leaving the Pennant estate at Eglwysbach to his sister's son, the Rev John Boulger, who served

The door to the Gwydir Chapel

Llanrwst, possibly while his uncle was acting as Canon of Westminster where he is buried. He was evidently much esteemed for J Williams in his history writes in 1830 that Llanrwst Church was 'officiated by our worthy Clergyman, the Rev J Boulger'.

A large brass on the wall of the vestry reads:

"In memory of the Rev John Boulger, MA of Pennant, only son of John Boulger Esq and Mary Holland-Boulger his wife. He died December 11th 1875 aged eighty-five and was buried December 17th in the Pennant Vault in Eglwysbach churchyard."

A search of Eglwys-bach churchyard failed to reveal any sign of his grave. There is also a small brass in the vestry to the Rev Edward Edwards MA, late rector who died in November 1756.

St Mary's chapel-of-ease, was built in 1842 by the subscriptions of 'a few pious individuals, for the benefit of English residents and a daily number of increasing visitors'. A handsome endowment was provided by a former rector, the Rev Holland-Edwards, Prebendary of Westminster. Despite a propitious start so that the church could be maintained, it was demolished in the late 1980s. Of particular interest is a memorial to Admiral John Wyatt Watling (1787-1868) who as a boy of fourteen was with the fleet at Nelson's capture of Copenhagen.

Publisher's note: The church has now been demolished.

A more ancient chapel-of-ease is at **Capel Garmon**, known as St Germain's Chapel. It was founded in pre-Reformation days and has been subjected to considerable rebuilding.

The parish contains the picturesque private chapel at Gwydir Uchaf which Sir Richard Wynn, 4th Baronet, built a year before his death. An unusual incumbent was William Brickdall who was a parliamentary appointment during the Commonwealth but at the Restoration was instituted by Bishop George Griffith. The name has several spellings but the signature in Llanrwst Register is 'Brickdall'. He was also Canon and Precentor of St Asaph Cathedral. Sir Owen had acquired a lease of the Llanrwst Vicarage and it was by his influence that Canon Brickdall obtained the living. In a letter to Sir Owen in February 1649, William Brickdall observes that although by civil law church livings may not be let for more than three years, yet by the law of civility, he is bound, although a churchman, to let himself to Sir Owen's service for ever, and he desires him to subscribe his name on the lease enclosed. This may appear irregular but it must be recalled that in 1646 the Episcopacy was abolished and the parliament claimed the right to appoint incumbents who satisfied their requirements. Brickdall's name appears frequently in the register. Sir Richard Wynn thought well of 'honest Brickdall' and terms him his 'good friend'.

THE PARISH REGISTERS 4

'We have three Register Books: The first from 1589 to 1628; the second from 1632 to 1691; the third from 1692 to this present year.'

So wrote the Rural Dean in 1729. The first, small, thin and damaged appears to have entries of value. The second register, about fourteen inches in length by eight in width is of heavy parchment. The front cover and first page are missing, the back cover is in ribbons, the writing is sometimes indecipherable. There are interesting Salusbury and Wynn entries. Nothing exists of the Civil War Years. The entries are in Latin and are a few selections:-

1634 Baptised Dorothy daughter of John Salusbury of Plas Isa, 11 July.

1637 Buried Margaret Wynne, als Mostyn, wife and widow of Hugh Wynne, Berth ddu, armiger, 16 May.

1639 Baptised Sidney (sic), daughter of Mr Owen Wynne of Gwydir, 16 October.

1639 Baptised Robert Wynne, son of Robert Wynne of Defferin and Dorothy his wife, 6 December.

1639 Buried Sydney Wynne, daughter of Owen Wynne of Gwydir and Grace his wife, 19 September.

1639 Baptised Jane, daughter of Maurice Wynne and Anne his wife, 26 January.

1640 Married Robert Trygarn and Grace vch David, 24 September.

1640 Buried Robert Wynne de Berthu, 24 February.

1641 Baptised Richard, son of Robert Trygarn and Grace his wife, 20 May.

1660 Buried Owen Wynne bart, of Gwydir, 13 August.

1660 Buried Hugo Jones MA, former Vicar of Llanrwst, 2 December.

1661 Baptised Mary, daughter of D Richard Wynne, baronet, of Gwydir.

1661 Buried John Salusbury of Plas Isa, armiger, 28 December.

1663 Buried David Lloyd of Hen-place, 24 October.

1663 Buried Ellen Wynne of Llanrwst. Died 8 January aged one hundred and thirteen years and buried 10 January. (signed William Bricknall, vicar)

1664 Buried Jane vch Robert Wynne, 8 April.

1664 Buried Dom: Jane Wynne, daughter of Robert Wynne, armiger of Berth ddu, 28 October.

1666 Buried Lowry Stanley of Llanrwst, 29 March.

1665 Married Peter Bodwell of Llyn in Caernarvonshire and Elizabeth (-Davies) of Llanrwst, 1 July.

1665 Married Hugh Lloyd of Rosyndall, Denbigh and Mary, 6 January.

1667 Baptised John, son of Richard Wynn of Gwydir, kt and bart, and Sara his wife, 22 October.

1667 Baptised Jane, daughter of Maurice Trygarn and Margaret his wife, 15 November.

1667 Buried Robert Wynn of Havod y Maydd, died at Llanelian and buried Llanrwst Church, 3 December.

1667 Buried John, son of D Richard Wynn of Gwydder (sic), kt and bart.

1668 Buried Dorothy, wife of William Bricknall, clr Vicar of Llanrwst died 9 December and buried 10.

1669 Married William Brickdall, clr Vicar of Llanrwst and Sydney Wynne of Llwyn, 14 October.

1669 Baptised Gwen, daughter of Caddr Wynne of Plastirion and Grace his wife, 9 December.

1670 Buried Maurice Wynn of Gwydir, armiger, 30 September.

1670 Baptised Grace, daughter of Cadwaladr Wynne, armiger, of Berthdu in Llanrwst Church, 24 July.

1670 Baptised Robert Salusbury of Plas Isa in Llangernew Church, 8 November.

1672 Buried Gwen, daughter of Kadwalader Wynne, armiger of Berthdu, in Llanrwst Church, 24 July.

1672 Baptised Grace, daughter of Maurice Trygarn and wife, 30 August.

1674 Buried Richard Wynne of Gwydir, Kt and bart.

1674 Buried Hugh Wynne of Berthdu, armiger, 16 December.

1674 Baptised John, son of John Salusbury of Caerbellan and Ann his wife, 2 January.

1675 Elizabeth Kyffin of Llanrwst, 24 April.

1675 Baptised Robert, son of William Ponsonbie of Llanrwst, 1 May.

1677 Baptised Mary, daughter of William Brickdall, Vicar of Llanrwst and Sydney his wife, 19 August.

1688 Baptised Robert, son of Evan Morris, pedlar of Garthgarmon and wife, 12 May.

1688 Baptised Elena, daughter of Edward Shone, ffidler and wife, 12 May.

1688 Buried daughter of Hugh Jones glou'r, 13 May.

1689 Buried Thomas Salusbury, 11 January.

1690 Baptised Robert, son of Robert Wynne of Berthdu, armiger, and Elena his wife, 9 July.

1691 Buried Robert Wynne of Berthdu, armiger, 27 July.

THE VESTRY BOOK

The name of Ellis Price of the Eagles is mentioned as a churchwarden in 1773. The following year a man was paid two guineas a year to rehearse for 'the encouragement of Psalm singers'.

In 1750 Wm Parry was employed as 'Vestry Clark' at ten shillings yearly for his trouble therein.

In 1781 the vestry dealt with another parishioner who was disordered in his senses and a dangerous person to be at liberty. 'Care must be taken with him at the expense of the Parish of Llanrwst either to send him to the mad house in Chester, else to have him bound in Chains of Iron with hand cuffs and to lodge him in some safe place and a strong person to look after him to bring him his diet etc.'

The coming of the turnpike road to the Ruthin district caused the vestry to invest in the new undertaking. They had a mortgage of two hundred and seventy five pounds and twelve shillings on the Llandegla Gate and one hundred pounds on the Llanrwst Gate. In 1783 it was ordered that the churchwardens proceed to raise a rate of six pence in the pound on the parishioners towards rebuilding Capel Garmon. For sometime it had been 'in decai'd condition'.

PESTILENCE

Periodically epidemics swept the town. In 1605 the Bishop of St Asaph received a report from Llanrwst that the church was too small for such a large parish and that it was 'pestered wth contunuall burialls' so that 'the area within is become pestylenciall and so noysome, that for a moneth space and more, most of the better sorte of the p(a)rishe refuse to come there and those that came were hardlie able to abyde hitt'.

An outbreak of typhus occurred in 1740 and people died so fast that 'in Llanrwst Church-yard there were at ye same time eleven graves open and nine at another time'.

A local man who played a prominent part in fighting disease and in developing Llanrwst's Public Health Services was Dr Owen Owen Roberts (1793-1866). He is buried in Eglwys-bach Churchyard in the tomb of his father William Lloyd Roberts of Cefn-y-coed, Maenan. Dr Roberts was educated in Llanrwst Grammar School and subsequently developed an extensive practice in the town. 'He was an eminent and versatile man in his day,' observes the late Mr H Parry Jones, 'a pioneer in health and municipal enterprise, a trenchant and even violent pamphleteer against feudalism in every form.'

The Wynn papers contain a number of allusions to epidemics, one going by the grim title of 'the great sickness'.

'The town of Llanrwst is small and ill built.' So writes Thomas Pennant about 1770.

The exposed interiors of the houses in Denbigh Street, demolished in the 1960s, revealed low ceilings, small windows, narrow doorways and passages, which all indicate the cramped living conditions of early days. These were the dwellings of traders and artisans who represented the greater proportion of the population. Most of the homes of the sixteenth and seventeenth century gentry are now farms. Many are of solid construction and though not imposing retain a quiet dignity, which bespeaks their origin.

John Williams, writing in 1830, endeavours to rectify Pennant's criticism of Llanrwst:

> 'The town is now neatly built, since nearly all the houses which Mr Pennant saw are rebuilt. It consists of five streets, four lanes and a large market square containing three hundred and forty two houses and one thousand four hundred and seventy seven inhabitants.'

When dealing with a period of which no consistent record survives it is necessary to construct something from fragmentary sources. Collections of estate papers include deeds and documents in which names of local persons and places are mentioned. At the University College of North Wales, for instance, are Mostyn Manuscripts which record Llanrwst property transactions. There is a reference in 1666 to a street 'leading from the cornmarket to the school'.

It is possible to reconstruct portions of the town as it was about 1666 and even if these fragments are disconnected they assist where no maps are available. Documents in the University College Library show that the early name for Station Road was Little Bridge Street. It is where the Afon Bach hurries to join the Conwy near Willow Street. From the south side of the square ran 'Street Bont Mawr'. Some property here is mentioned in the Mostyn MSS in 1723. A mortgage was granted to Thomas Kyffin Esq and Robert Wynne of Bodysgallen Esq on a close called Tyddyn Cae-y-graig, a house with gardens called Pen-y-bont and another house also with gardens named Crosskeys.

There is a reference in 1789 to a street called Street y Pwll. Sir Roger Mostyn granted thirty years lease on five newly-erected houses on the north side of the street. Between a brook called Nant Goron was a tenement called Bwlch-y-gwynt near another tenement where Hugh ap John ap Meredith, weaver, dwelt, beside the land of Sir Richard Wynne, bart, known as Rhyd-yr-efail on the north side. This is revealed in a mortgage granted by Robert

Wynne of Berth-ddu and William David of Tŷ-brith Ucha, yeoman, to one Owen David Lloyd of Mathebrwd, gent, in 1639-40.

In 1630 a fulling mill in encountered 'standing upon a close named Kae yr pandy'. There is the 'sign of the Spread Eagle' in 1719 and the Cross Keys is also mentioned.

A six month lease for Berth-ddu was drawn up in 1735 between Robert Wynne of Bodysgallen Esq and James Conway of Cotton Hall, gent, and William Evans of Berth-ddu, gent. This indicates that the Wynns' long occupation of Berth-ddu was terminating but greater interest lies in place-names. There is 'a mansion and garden in Street y Bont, probably the Glan Conwy marked on the OS map of 1875. Also a water corn mill called Y Felin Isa. A kiln is named, also 'yr hen efel alias the Old Smithy and Pen y bont alias the horns'. A document of 1680 alludes to 'a house, premises and garden called Tu David Morris the weaver' and a house and premises in 'the street leading from the towne to the bridge where John Griffith, tanner now dwells'.

In 1789 Sir Roger Mostyn (2nd Baronet) granted a twenty-one years' lease to Ellen Roberts, widow, on land on the north side of a bridge in Llanrwst called 'y bont bach' on the east side of the highroad – now Station Road – leading from Llanrwst to Tal-y-cafn. The old name for Station Road was Stryd Bont Afon bach. This refers to the new toll road constructed down the east side of the Conwy River. Another lease concerns 'five newly erected houses on the north side of a street called Street y Pwll'.

Thanks to the Hearth Tax of 1662 it is possible to catch another glimpse of the early town. The official statistics are in the Public Records Office and a copy has been supplied by the National Library of Wales. Only six of the townships are represented. Gwydir township was on the west side of the river and contained few houses. The picture which is created of Llanrwst is that of a few homes of the gentry on the perimeter and a huddle of little dwellings, each with one hearth (or no hearth at all) in the heart of the town. The Act taxes 'hearth or stoves'. Separate columns distinguish between houses to be taxed and those which pay no tax. The Lady Grace Wynn was taxed for six hearths. This would be Cae'r Melwr where she retired after Sir Owen's death in 1660.

Mr Thomas Salusbury, five hearths, obviously indicates Plas Isa. John Salusbury of Plas Isa, armiger, was buried 28 December 1663 and Thomas, his son, succeeded him. Hugh Wynne, Esquire with eight hearths must be Colonel Hugh Wynn who left Bodysgallen after the war to dwell in the ancestral home, Berth-ddu. Mr William Brigdall, three hearths, is the rector. The house with nine hearths might be Plas Tirion as the owner is Robert Wynne, Esquire. Other names include John Owen, gent, three hearths in Mathebrwyd township; Robert Lloyd, two hearths in Llanddoged; Mr Thomas Wynne, three in Garthgarmon; Robert Hughes, four in Trybrith Isa; Mr Wm Kyffin, two in Garthgyfanedd township. He was probably the heir of Maenan as the Kyffins owned land in this area. Houses totalled one hundred and sixty seven and of those one hundred and thirty eight were of one hearth only. Seventy houses paid no tax. Totals in each township are:-

Townships	Over three	Three	Two	One	Not taxed
Llanrwst	3	3	2	24	34
Garthgarmon	-	1	4	43	9
Tybrith Isa	2	3	1	28	-
Llanddoged	-	1	1	14	13
Mathebrwyd	-	2	5	16	5
Garthgyfannedd	-	-	1	13	9
Total	5	10	14	138	70

Edward Lhwyd in 1699 estimated that Llanrwst had sixty-six houses. He lists, in his quaint spelling, the townships as: Tre Lan Ryst, Garth Gyvannedh, Malhebrwd, Ty bruth Ycha, Garth Garmon (all in Denbighshire) and Trewydyr (Caernarvonshire). He mentions ten bridges and names twenty-one houses of consequence with their owners. The first (as might be expected) was Gwydir then owned by Lord Willoughby de Eresby. Next comes 'Berthy' belonging to 'Mr Robt Wynn of Bodyskelhan', a minor aged nine. This is confirmed by the Church Register which enters the baptism of Robert, son of Robert Wynne of Berth-ddu, armiger, and Elena his wife, 9 July 1690.

Other houses are:

"3. Plas Tirion, Cadwaladr Wyn of Voelas Esq.

4. Plas Isa, belonging to Mr Robert Salusbury Ll b Coll Jesu Oxon.

5. Y plas yn Rhos, William Anwyl Gent whose son is Mr Rys Anwyl.

6. Plas Ycha belongs to Mr Kyffin of Maynan whose mother lives there.

7. Brynniog, Mr Hugh Lloyd, his son Gruff: now at Jes Coll, Oxon.

8. Y Lhwyne belongs to Mr Thelwal of Nant Clwyd, who lately purchased it from Mr Wynn.

9. Mathebrwyd (mae rhiw enw aralh yw dy vo) Mr Robert Thomas.

10. Garthebog (q an Garth hebog) a berthyn i vab Owen Davydh and Sir Veirionydh, yr Owen D ymma a briodh Wyres ag Aeres i Dommas.

11. Y Kyfdy als yr Hendre John Elis.

12. Yr Hendre; Rich Davies

13. Rhiw'r maen brith. Robt Sion ap Elis Prys.

14. Maes y Garnedh John Jones o Ddinbech a briodedh Vlaens Salbri.

15. Rhyd Lan Vair Mr John Humphreys, Minister of Eglwys Vach lately dec who left issue.

16. Keven Kestilk: Hugh ap William.

17. Plas Newydh belongs to Sir Rich Midlton.

18. Yr Orsedh Wen Wm Morris Maurice.

19. Karreg y vran belongs to Rhobert Sion Elis.

20. Kae'r Melwr belongs to Gwydir.

21. Kae'r Berlhan John Williams."

Some of these names have clearly altered over the years or reflect a lack of a standard form of spelling at the time.

Reference is made to 'Cay-r-Berllan in Trybrith Issa' in 1642 when it was occupied by Robert Hughes, gent.

Further indication of growth in the following century is to be found in the Episcopal Visitation returns. Extracts are:

1738 'It is thought that we have about four hundred families within our parish.'

1753 'I think the number of families in the parish that pay parish rates may be about two hundred and twenty besides a great number who live in huts.'

1791 'It (the parish) contains in all near a thousand or more dwelling houses.'

1795 'It comprehends upwards of six hundred houses.'

Vague estimating could not continue indefinitely and in 1801 a census return for the entire country was taken. Llanrwst's figures are:-

1801 2,549	1851 3602	1901 4591	1951 2596
1811 2502	1861 3593	1911 2519	1961 2562
1821 2986	1871 3767	1821 2484	1971 2743
1831 3231	1881 4260	1931 2475	1981 2903
1841 3524	1891 4964	1941 War	1991 3070
			2000 3140

(*2001 figures not available*)

The Napoleonic War was in progress during this period. From 1831 to 1851 the population increased by three hundred and seventy one. From 1861 to 1881 the increase was six hundred and sixty seven. It would seem that the coming of the railway contributed to this advance. Llanrwst became an urban district on 1st January 1897 under the Act of 1894.

Old dwellings are disappearing as area after area is demolished. To glimpse the Llanrwst of long ago, to comprehend something of the way the humble families lived, it is necessary to wander down alleys or explore remote corners where a few forlorn homes linger in decrepitude, silently speaking of days which hold an attraction only when viewed dispassionately from a distance, mellowed by time.

The place which probably excites the imagination most, is the insignificant passage which runs beside the former Electricity Showrooms, now La Barrica Restaurant in Ancaster Square. Now elegantly alluded to as London Terrace, it once bore the mysterious designation of Steam Packet Entry. The name must have become distorted for there can be no logical connection with a steam packet in this part of the river. The first steam packet to ply between Liverpool and North Wales did not sail until about 1820. Any person who has seen a picture of the vessel – the Cambrian – with huge paddle-wheels and a smokestack higher than the mast might doubt whether she could get as far as Conwy Quay let alone make her way up river, particularly after Telford's bridge was built.

There can be little doubt about the usefulness of this short cut between the busy square and the riverside. Modern buildings replace those of David Cox's day when he painted them more than a century ago. But once the rear of the shops is passed a different world is entered. Two stone houses, sturdily built but incredibly small, remain to show what a 'semi-detached' of those days looked like. Each has a kitchen – a *cegin*. Above is a tiny bedroom approached by a staircase set against the dividing wall. Farther down the uneven walk is another type, approached by several steps leading to the only door. The north wall of the churchyard may be seen rising high above the squat dwellings. Masonry checks further progress but it is obvious that these later erections block a way that led to the river bank where there was probably a landing place, perhaps used only by rowing boats. Another narrow winding passage is one which runs from the zebra crossing in the Square to Watling Street. Here again, long ago, many small houses would have clustered. It would be in this vicinity, one surmises, that the Llanrwst Constable was murdered in 1604 by the 'swaggering' gentlemen.

There are insufficient references in the vestry books and registers to form a 'trade dictionary' of those days but a few names collected do confirm some of the occupations one would expect to find. From what Sir John Wynn wrote in a memo there was a tannery in his day and there was probably one much earlier as leather was indispensable, not merely for footwear but for harness. The late Mr Norman Rogers Jones recalls that the Tannery – Plas Helig – was once owned by a Mr David Davies who lived at Pen-isa-dre, or Plas-yn-dre, which was demolished to make way for the Police Station.

'It is stated that he would not sell any of the cattle hides that he cured at the works for about five years. The hide was then as hard as a zinc sheet. Consequently when men's boots were made, or soled-and-heeled, the leather was so stiff that they lasted for months and months. I was told by Mr Edward Mills who took over the works on the death of Mr David Davies that they had all their dyes from Germany so that when the First World War broke out these dyes were impossible to obtain and the firm had to rely on a supply of dyes from England.'

The town had a variety of industries. References are encountered to a foundry, tannery, brewery, dye-works, rope-works, which contrasted with more delicate occupations such as glove making, the manufacture of harps and grandfather clocks. Furniture was made for domestic use or for sale. Many of the carved mantelpieces in the homes of the gentry would be the work of craftsmen on the estates. The sturdy construction of many houses testifies to suitable quarries in the vicinity.

The old Chandlery in Church Walks was working 'in full swing' within living memory. The Chandlery, now demolished, turned towards the river and abutted on Bridge Street. It had stables, coach house and a cottage, all of which have been taken down.

One of the last 'nailers' in the district died in Llanrwst as late as the 20th Century. Owen Davies had his workshop off Denbigh Street and here he shaped hand-made nails as in olden days.

The registers are disappointing and rarely give occupations but from various sources some names have been picked out. Encountered are Richard the weaver; John Thomas, ffeltmaker (1636); Hugh Jones and Harry John, glovers; Hugh Davies, smith; Thomas Davies described as 'mercator' (map maker?) and (1664) Hugh ap Evan who is termed 'Coriarius'. Also were: harper, mercer, labourer, miller, saddler, excise officer. There was a 'medicus' at Gwydir in Stuart times. Beside the path to the church is the grave of a harp-maker, the instrument being depicted on the slab. (see p. 49)

Llanrwst was celebrated for its harp-makers and its harpers. There are tombstones to Thomas Parry, 'Harper of this town', who died in 1791 and David Roberts, 'merchant and harper' who died in 1779. In the churchyard also rest the remains of Robert Williams, 'Trebor Mai' (an eminent poet) who died in 1877.

On fair days, cattle were sold in the market square in the morning and horses in the afternoon.

The *Weekly News* of 23 February 1939, issued a supplement on the district which included an old photograph of part of the square. There was no HSBC Bank (erected in 1870), its site being occupied by a row of cottages (see p. 71). Two well-known local characters were in the foreground, 'Captain Toby Robin' and 'Robin Business'. An old woman carrying a bucket is said to be on her way to Llandudno to get seawater for her rheumatism.

Northern-bound motorists after turning from the Square to enter Station Road have no time to glance at the little entry known as Willow Street. The now incongruous name suggests the proximity of the river and doubtless was bestowed in less strenuous days when such trees ringed the riverbank. This is now a quiet area but it once represented the heart of the town's activity. Here, side by side, stood Llanrwst's brewery and Llanrwst's tannery. A pedestrian who explores Willow Street will come upon a high, dignified building of grey stone which appears strangely out of place in the present setting. This was once the Brewery House where once dwelt the once well-known Elias family. A covered archway leads to the rear premises where there may still be seen the cobbled road once worn smooth by the hoofs of the powerful dray-horses. The buildings are now adapted for commercial purposes. Between the house and the churchyard opposite lies the old walled garden. Further westward was the tannery, actively employed untill 1979.

Despite changed conditions this quiet corner of the town still retains an atmosphere of bygone days. A memo of Sir John Wynn, on 23 June 1597, reads:

'Repair the tanning house and lease it to a tanner'.

There is no indication of where the place stood. It might have been on this site near the church as a vestry in 1729 records that skins had been hung on the churchyard yews and the churchwardens were instructed to notify the tanner and skinners that unless they were removed they would be flung in the river. The tannery was started by Mr David Davies of Plas-yn-dre and dates from 1875. The next owner was Mr Edward Mills. In the 1960s it was owned by Mr Smith who stated that before being established in its present position it was in Plas Isa.

THE OLD BREWERY

Mr Elias writes: when the brewery started I do not know. Mr Thomas Elias took it over from a Mr Williams in 1875 and it closed down in 1905 four years after Mr Elias's death. Part of the brewery is now a factory. A description of the building which stood between the churchyard wall and the river has been supplied by Mr Perys Elias, of Penmaenmawr, son of Mr Thomas Elias.

'The brewery had two storeys. At the top was a space for sugar and a large deep vat into which the sugar (which looked like hard butter) was emptied from iron containers suspended from chains. On the first floor was a second vat and it was in this vat that the excise man tested the 'content' of the beer on brew days. In another part was a long shallow vat, probably for cooling off the beer. Not far from that was a small vat, the lower part of which extended to the ground floor. This was only occasionally used, probably for surplus beer. The ground floor contained Mr Elias's small office. In another part, down some steps, was a door overlooking a stream. In time of flood this part of the ground floor was generally under water as was the adjoining cellar of the brewery house.

Opposite the entrance stood a low wagon, which was used to hold the dregs left after a brewing. This was called a 'soweg' and poor people used to collect portions for pig food. At some distant time the brewery had been attached to a farm, or a farm connected with the brewery, as there were two barns. At the back of the large barn was a small field used by pigs and ducks. In time of flood, river and tributary overflowed and swept up Willow Street to the main road.'

Mr Elias said that for twenty years the brewery thrived but began to decline after the death of the chief brewer, John Jones, an expert at his job and a regular attender at chapel. 'He never touched beer himself,' added Mr Elias. Opposite to the brewery was their garden and orchard. The chief brewer lived in a semi-detached house, which was connected with the brewery. On one occasion, when they had their greatest flood, the ground floor was swamped and breakfast had to be served upstairs. A timely warning enabled the carpets to be saved.

> 'The beer was taken up country to Pentrevoelas, Llangernwy, Penmachno and Yspytty by horse and cart. The vehicle had long back-boards with chains, which enabled the casks to be unloaded. The carter was popularly known as Tommy Cefn, a stalwart who played cricket and football for the town.'

Mr Elias remembered the night when Lewis's timber yard caught fire and as it was near the gasometer there was fear of an explosion. Many inhabitants made for the hills. 'The fire lit up the district but fortunately was brought under control. Quite a feat for the local fire brigade in those days.'

Mr Elias was fortunate in being present in Ancaster Square on two conspicuous occasions; the first, when the Colonial Premiers were visiting this country for Queen Victoria's Diamond Jubilee in 1897. A photograph shows Sir Wilfred Laurier, Premier of Canada, speaking in the square. Lord and Lady Carrington are on his left and the Premiers of Australia's states and New Zealand are seated behind the speaker. The next occasion was the visit of the Duke and Duchess of York (later King George V and Queen Mary) to Gwydir.

TIMBER MERCHANTS

The first timber merchants, P & H Lewis, played an important part in the life of the town, particularly as they established a branch at Conwy, to which harbour timber from the Baltic countries was brought in three-masted ships. These vessels were a familiar sight in the estuary early last century. The firm had, in addition to Conwy Quay, a large depot in Llanrwst, which is still known as Lewis Yard.

> 'There were a large number employed,' writes Mr Elias, 'Mr Peter Lewis died while quite young, leaving four daughters and one son. The latter died while quite a young man in his teens. The business was a very large one. They used to purchase timber in the district. They also bought huge balks of all kinds of foreign wood. About a dozen horses of the biggest, strongest, shire breed were kept (17.2 hands). The other brother in the firm was Mr Humphrey Lewis and he managed the Conway branch. The large foreign balks of timber were brought up river in small steamers from Conway to Trefriw. Then the timber wagons with four or six horses carried the load to Plough Street in Llanrwst.'

Mr Ifor E Davies discovered that Mr Watkin Lewis had a ship called the *John Pegg* built at Trefriw in 1858. In Seion (Calvinistic Methodist) Chapel in Llanrwst is a pulpit made by P & H Lewis at their timber-yard. It is fashioned out of pine, in keeping with the rest of the interior. The firm was noted for its good work and long service of its workmen.

THE FOUNDRY

The foundry was situated in Denbigh Street and was established and worked for many years by two brothers, John and Richard Thomas, blacksmiths, who, in addition to the foundry, had two blacksmith's shops. One shop was situated in Denbigh Street opposite to The Walk and the other at the opposite end of the town, Tal-y-bont. This became a grocer's shop known by its former designation as 'Yr Efail'.

The Foundry was a large place employing many men. They were experienced moulders and fashioned all kinds of wrought-iron implements – ploughs, crushing-machines, drain and manhole covers or seat frames such as seen on the promenade of Llandudno and Colwyn Bay.

'We boys knew which day the smelting took place and if allowed watched the white molten steel and iron ore pouring from the furnace into the mould bucket and from there to the moulds made in the sand where the moulds were designed and made.'

The horseshoeing business was very important. Many of the blacksmiths were renowned and won prizes at the premier agricultural show in the country. There were hundreds of shire horses in the district in 1900. It was one of the best known areas for shire horses, also harness and hackney horses, ponies and cobs.

THE WALK AND ROPE WORKS

The Walk would have derived its name from the covered way or walk used by rope man-ufacturers when fibres were twisted into rope. The establishment of a rope, twine and hemp merchant was begun in the eighteenth century at a place called 'The Walk', observed Mr Norman Rogers-Jones:

'This was the field on the south side of Denbigh Street near to Henar, a doctor's house and opposite the blacksmith's shop in the same street. It was founded by William Jones (1792-1877) who was William Jones-Davies but he dropped the Davies. His wife was known as Beti Williams. They had many children but only one, John, followed in the business, as a rope-maker and hemp merchant. When ropes were manufactured by machinery the business faded away. John Jones was apprenticed to his father during the reign of King William IV. The indenture made between father and son is a most interesting document. I have the indenture at home as old William Jones of Bodunig was my great-great-grandfather. After the decline of the rope and twine business William Jones did well as a timber merchant. He married the daughter of a Thomas and Jane Rogers of Trefriw. Mr and Mrs Rogers kept a shop. They also had a slate quarry at Llanrhychwyn abutting on the Crafnant Road and a lime kiln on the quay at Trefriw. He had his quarry working full time and the small steamers from Conwy came up to Trefriw to collect the slates; these brought cargoes of limestone, possibly from the Ormeshead quarries. He also ran the post office.'

His slate quay is shown on page 89. His daughters were well-read girls. One produced a Welsh book in 1813, which enabled a Welsh child of those days to read his bible. She was an excellent first-aider and was equal to any doctor. As a family they used to go over the mountains on the backs of their ponies to Gerlan, Bethesda, to communion service once a month. Their son John Jones was the father of Thomas Rogers-Jones, father of Norman Rogers-Jones. A granddaughter of William Jones married Ebenezer Rees, Llansannan, whose brother was William Rees (Gwilym Hiraethog).

LONG-CASE CLOCKS

During the eighteenth and nineteenth centuries Llanrwst seems to have been a centre of watch and clockmaking. One of the clockmakers most frequently encountered is Moses Evans who began his work at Llangernyw before the second half of the eighteenth century. In 1780 he moved to Llanddoged. Many clocks belong to this period. They are of the long-case brass dial variety. Later in life he moved to Llanrwst, possibly to retire, suggests the Rev George Metcalfe who so generously supplied me with most of this information on clockmakers in the town. Moses Evans was so industrious that some collectors believe that there were two men of that name at work.

One of John Owen's clocks

Again we must be grateful to the Rev George Metcalfe:

'Little wonder that Moses Evans's clocks are far by the most numerous in North Wales today. He began work at Llangernyw before 1750 for there is a clock in Dolwen inscribed 1751. Between 1780 and 1819 he appears to have been in business in Llanddoget. He then moved to Llanrwst, possibly to retire, but even here he could not be idle and one long-case clock of this period has been recorded at Llansannan and several at Llandudno.'

Another Moses Evans long-case clock was seen by the writer at the home of Mrs Cecil Morgan, Frondirion, near Criccieth. It has a magnificent mahogany case and still keeps excellent time in spite of many a 'Chwalfa fawr'. This clock has been in the family for over one hundred and fifty years. It is interesting to note that this clock was for many years in Llanrwst Rectory, now Glan-y-borth, when Canon John Lloyd Morgan was the incumbent during the early part of the 20th century.

A John Owen, clockmaker of Llanrwst, made the old Town Clock of Llanrwst. The dial has been preserved by the council. A long-case clock bearing his name is dated 1755. Among the Denbigh Street craftsmen were John Roberts, Robert Roberts, Rowland Griffiths and in Little Bridge Street there was Theophilus Davies.

A Watkin Owen of Llanrwst followed his trade in the town from 1761 to 1809 and several specimens of his work are in the National Museum of Wales. The Rev George Metcalfe possesses a beautiful silver watch dated 1790 inscribed Watkin Owen, Llanrwst. It still keeps excellent time. Many of his clocks are still in use today and he was one of four generations of the family who made clocks from at least 1702 onwards.

Another Owen, William Owen, practised in Denbigh Street in 1835. A silver watch he made is in the National Library of Wales. Humphrey Owen made long-case clocks in Denbigh Street in 1844. Towards the close of the nineteenth century Llanrwst clockmakers endeavouring to compete with the cheap watches which followed the Free Trade Acts, cut their own wheels and pinions and cast other parts at the local foundry. Another long-cased inlaid clock seen by the writer at Gwernfor, Llanrwst, was made by Barker and Son of Llanrwst.

PRINTING

Llanrwst acquired more than local fame in the printing world by the ingenuity of John Jones whose 'Printing Office' sign was a familiar sight for many years. His grandfather, Dafydd Jones, 1703-85, attracted attention by setting up a permanent printing works in Trefriw in 1776. His son, Ishmael Jones removed to Llanrwst. It was the latter's son John Jones, who made a name for himself by his enterprise. He made his own machines and cut his own type. Some of the hand-cut type was remarkably minute and books printed in this were a rare novelty. Under the name of Venedotian Press, he published extensively and became probably the most famous publisher in Wales. The writer possesses an insignificant looking book published by John Jones, Llanrwst, in 1830. It measures six inches by three and a half inches. It is John Williams' *Faunula Grustensis*, 'an outline of the natural contents of the Parish of Llanrwst'. It contains a brief history of the town, its commerce and agriculture and in particular, a catalogue in Latin, English and Welsh of the animals and plants. Modest though the one hundred and forty eight page booklet appears it was the work of a local man who was so gifted that he attained a post on the staff of Kew Gardens. When the printing works closed down in 1936 much of the equipment was presented to the Science Museum in South Kensington where some of it is on exhibition in the 'Printing Collection'. The remainder is in store. The Science Museum have kindly sent the list of the main items:-

Ruthven type press, baling press, lead cutting machine, lead moulds, paper cutting machine, wood types, wood blocks, embossing and bookbinding tools, hand-made patrices and matrices, ladles, chases and galleys, composing sticks and some set-up pages for the *Holyhead Almanac*.

HOSIERY

Knitting stockings for sale remained a centuries-old occupation. Residents can recall seeing women seated on stools in the Square, industriously knitting while awaiting customers to purchase from baskets of apples and oranges which they had brought to Llanrwst. Samuel Lewis in 1833 wrote:

> 'Llanrwst was formerly noted for the making of harps; at present the spinning of woollen yarn and the knitting of stockings constitute the principle branches of trade, the town being situated at the north-western extremity of the hosiery district of North Wales and next to Bala, the principal market for that article.'

Lewis adds that the town was supplied with coal, lime, timber and groceries brought to Trefriw in vessels of sixty tons. They carried back the produce of slate quarries and mines in the adjoining parishes.

HARP-MAKERS AND HARPISTS

The following section dealing with the harp-makers of Llanrwst was generously prepared by Mr Robert Jones, BSc, JP, to whom my grateful acknowledgement is made.

There have been in the district famous harpists like Dafydd Maenan, Tomos Anwyl and others. Although Robert Griffith, in his book 'Cerdd Dannau', did much pioneering work on the history of Llanrwst harp-makers he failed to trace further back than 1650.

Llanrwst was definitely on the map as a small town famous for its harp-makers as early as the end of the seventeenth century and William Camden, the well-known travelling historian, mentions this in his Camden's Britannia, but this cannot be traced earlier than the time of Elizabeth. Fortunately in manu 63, Cardiff Corporation Library, there is a Cywydd composed by Dafydd ab Llewelyn ap Madog asking for a harp from Gruffydd Coetmor, grandson of Hywel Coetmor, who lived in Cefel Castle in Coetmor, parish of Llanrwst – the old castle belonging to Peredur ap

Efrawg, according to Gruffydd Hiraethog. It is well known that Hywel was one of the famous captains in the Battle of Agincourt, 1415; he had a son called Dafydd ab Hywel who sold his estate, Gwydir, to Maredydd ap Ieuan from Gesail Gyfarch. Gruffydd Coetmor was his son. He flourished round about 1450 to 1480 and doubtless he carried out his important craft round about 1400.

According to the Cywydd it appears that he was an expert harp-maker and that he possessed a gift for the work. He could gild the letters, carve the wood, join the three timbers of the harp and prepare the wood and he showed himself to be a clever craftsman.

About one hundred and twenty years later Peilyn lived in the Llanrwst area; he was also an able harp-maker and a good harpist. Huw Machno and others about 1570 to 1620 describe him.

Robert Griffith says that a Telyn deires (triple-harp) was shown in an exhibition in Llanrwst in 1891 and carved on its soundboard were the words 'Manufactured in Llanrwst 1610'. At the same time another Telyn deires was shown there, the property of Colonel Wynne-Finch of Voelas, and this had also been made in Llanrwst.

A Telyn un-thes (single harp) once the property of William Owen, Pencraig, was made in the Llanrwst district. Made of sycamore (mesarn) it was four foot nine inches high and had thirty-three strings and was the type of the Elizabethan period. William ap Owen of Pencraig was buried in Llanrwst Churchyard in January 1684. The air, 'Conset William Owen, Pencraig', keeps his name alive. Dafydd Cadwaladr, about 1650, belonged to the same old school of harpists, which was famous in Llanrwst long before John Richard became prominent in the craft.

Dafydd Morris, Dolgam, near the border of Llanrwst parish was a carpenter. He made a harp for his own amusement and this verse refers to him:

'Telyn wen yn llawn o dane
Wnaed yng nghoed y Glyn yn rhywle
Ac mae'n rhaid fod honno'n hwylus
O waith dwylaw Dafydd Morris.'

Translated:

'A white harp with many strings
Was made somewhere in Coed-y-Glyn
And it must be a useful one
Made by the hands of Dafydd Morris.'

The letters D M carved on an old building on Dolgam bear the date 1695. It was called the 'white' harp because the wood was unvarnished and had not been coloured.

Llanrwst was regarded as a famous centre for its harps during the eighteenth century and John Richard, born in the King's Head in 1711, was a specialist. William Jones, another craftsman, lived during the same period. Ifan from London taught John Richard as an apprentice. There is an entry in the Parish Register of baptisms referring to him and his wife, Catrin, having their son John baptised on 27 May 1744. He was called John Richard of Mallesbury and this indicated that he lived in England for some time.

He was in Llanrwst from 1744 to 1759. It was in 1755 that he made a triple harp for John Parry, the famous blind harpist from Ruabon. There was no other harp that could be compared with this because of its expert craftsmanship and the sweetness of its tone.

Soon afterwards his fame spread throughout Wales and he was regarded as the leading harp-maker in the country. He was invited to live in the palace of Sackville Gwynne, Esquire, in Glan

Brân near Llanymyddyfri (Llandovery) and he remained there for years as a harp-maker for that patriotic gentleman. He died there in 1789 and it is stated on his gravestone that he had the honour of being employed by Queen Charlotte to make harps. Sackville Gwynne promoted arrangements to bring the triple-harp (Telyn deires) into more general use in South Wales. During his stay in the palace John Richard made twenty of these harps and Gwynne presented them free to the harpists.

In auctions during the past one and a half centuries there was great excitement when John Richard's harps were for sale. The famous Wil Penmorfa used one of his harps in the mansions of South Wales families until the Delyn Bedol (Shoe Harp) came into more common use. The harp of the famous John Roberts is the one shown in the National Museum and this was made by John Richard. Ellis Roberts (Eos Merion) harpist to the Prince of Wales, played on some of his harps. Sir Robert Vychan, Nannau, possessed two of them and these were used during the first half of the last century by the well-known harpist of Dolgellau. William Pritchard of the Goat Hotel, Caernarfon, sold one of John Richard's biggest harps in a wooden case in 1811 for thirty-one guineas. Another of his harps was sold by him for twenty-four guineas. Considering the depreciation in the value of money, it is seen that John Richard's harps were highly regarded and considered to be of extraordinary high value. Their excellence was acclaimed publicly by such famous people as Lady Llanofer, Carnhuanawc, and the chief dealers in harps in London. John Richard left his mark noticeably on his Telyn deires in Wales and he himself made most of them in his time.

There were others, at that time, skilled in the same craft, like David Roberts, merchant and harp-maker, who died in Liverpool in 1779 when forty-eight years of age. He came from Melin-y-Coed. Dafydd Roberts, Caergeiliog, was his relation. The latter lived about 1780-1820 and was a clever craftsman with wood and famous as a harp-maker. David Roberts the merchant has been buried in Llanrwst Churchyard not far from the cemetery gates and a picture of a harp has been carved on the gravestone. This David Roberts must have been of some status otherwise the task of carving the picture of a harp would not have been undertaken.

Hugh Thomas, shoemaker, said in 1871 that no harps were made in Llanrwst after 1823. He remembered two harp-

The grave of David Roberts

makers, Dafydd Caergeiliog and Rowland Griffith. Dafydd lived in the almshouses and made his harps there. He did not like to finish his harps in the almshouses in case the noise of the old wife or his other neighbours went into the instrument to spoil the tone.

Another clever craftsman whose harps were in great demand was Rowland Griffith. He was a skilful carpenter and was also an expert at making wooden tobacco boxes. Thomas Roberts, Caergeiliog, was a capable harp-maker. He lived during the middle of the eighteenth century and like his brother Dafydd he could 'make a mill and grind in it and make a harp and play on it'.

The last harp-maker in Llanrwst was James Hughes, born in Ysqubor Gerrig near Trefriw and Llanrwst. He taught some of the most prominent harpists in Gwynedd and was an expert of the Telyn dier-thes (sic) and Telyn Bedol. He was competent at harp-making and in 1874 he played in an Eisteddfod at Llanrwst on a harp made by himself.

THE FREE SCHOOL

As the result of an endowment obtained from the rectorial title of Eglwysbach by Sir John Wynn, 1st Baronet, a Free School was erected in 1610. With the school went an almshouse and weekly lecture, the peculiar amalgamation being named the Jesus Hospital. It was stipulated that pupils from Eglwysbach, Llanrwst and Dolwyddelan must not be charged for their education; later a small fee was required from pupils from other areas. The school was described by John Williams in 1830:

'At the east end of the town, near a row of large walnut trees, is the School bank; this school, called the Free School, was erected about the same time and for similar purposes as the almshouses. The institution has until lately been wholly neglected, but now under the encouraging auspices of the Right Honourable Lord Willoughby de Eresby and the active exertions of the present Master and Mistress, it is become an excellent school and likely to be inferior to none in Wales.'

The Rural Dean of 1727 comments that the headmaster was Mr John Kendrick AB whose salary was twenty pounds per annum:

'He is a very industrious man and has sent some scholars to the university and has seventy or eighty boys under his tuition and his usher's. The headmaster lived in a house which adjoined the school to which was attached a garden and a field worth five pounds. Mr Kendrick acted as a curate for St Germain's Chapel at Capel Garmon. The Usher was Mr John Jones BA who was sober and industrious and had a wife and two children.'

The Rural Dean of 1749 contributes the information that the second master received eight pounds a year with house and garden and a further five pounds for reading prayers in the chapel. At this period Mr John Jones was headmaster with Mr Edward Edwards as second master.

It was claimed at one time that a John Williams, goldsmith to James I, had a share in founding the school. On two occasions the school was the subject of lawsuits and on one occasion was closed for several years. When the school celebrated its three hundred and fiftieth anniversary in 1960 a former headmaster, the late Mr H Parry Jones, wrote an account of the school for the Denbighshire Historical Society. It was also included by Mr A H Willams in his article on 'Old Endowed Grammar Schools'.

Mr Parry Jones observed that while it was clear that Sir John provided for school, almshouses and lectures by the tithes of Eglwys-bach, a point at issue was whether these funds constituted an endowment to support the school and almshouse, or whether the money was charitably given by the Gwydir family. Twice the Court of Chancery had to wrestle with the problem; once in 1678 and again in 1839. The first case arose when the Gwydir family declined to pay the headmaster and usher who claimed three hundred pounds arrears. The school had been apparently closed for a time and the usher's house turned into an inn. No decision was made by the court. The school was closed (1817 to 1828), the almshouses were rented or left empty. The court declared that there had been an endowment since 1610. In 1851 the school was reorganised and started a career, with a Grammar School curriculum. The headmaster had to be a graduate and a clerk in Holy Orders.

Mr Parry Jones points out that it was an old Grammar School boy, Dr O O Roberts who (with his brother) was chiefly responsible for the action of 1839. In 1879 a new scheme was framed by the Charity Commissioners. The title was changed to 'The Hospital School Foundation of Sir John Wynne of Gwydir'. In 1896 the old Grammar School became the new County School.

Among the scholars produced by Llanrwst Grammar School was Edward William Byron Nicholas who when thirty-three was appointed Librarian of the Bodleian Library. His father, a naval officer, died when Edward was a child and his mother, a sister-in-law of Admiral Sir Thomas Williams, brought her son to Llanrwst where, after attending a kindergarten school, he was admitted to Llanrwst Grammar School. He then went to Liverpool College where he won a scholarship for Trinity College, Oxford.

WORKHOUSE

To judge by Llanrwst vestry-books the town's administration changed but little from the memorable act of 1601 which amongst other things made each parish responsible for the care of its poor and ailing. The Elizabethan Act was expensive to administer and frequently caused disputes between adjoining parishes. With a more advanced form of living the system called for revision and in 1834 the Poor Law Act was remodelled. Duplicating of officials was rectified by grouping the parish into a 'Union' administered by a Board of Guardians. Each union had a workhouse, the upper part of the Conwy Valley being served by one in Llanrwst which stood near Plas isa dre at the north end of the town, no great walking distance from Conwy which catered for the lower part of the vale. Llanrwst Union was mostly in Denbighshire, but Dr A H Dodd points out that it included the seven southern parishes of Arllechwedd and four eastern parishes of Eifionydd.

The workhouse owed its name to the work able-bodied men were made to undertake in return for their board. Tramps making their way from one workhouse to another are no longer a familiar sight on the roads, as workhouses disappeared with the National Health Service.

Later it became a home for the aged known as Dolanog House. It stood near the railway station. The 'Union Workhouse' marked on the O S Map of 1875 shows a block of buildings alongside the goods yard from which it was separated by a row of trees. No sign of the building remains, its stout masonry having been utilised for other public work. Most of the demolition was carried out late in 1964.

THE POST OFFICE

There is evidence that a postal service to Llanrwst existed in Stuart times but details of how it operated are not available. There were post offices at Denbigh, St Asaph and Conwy, probably in the leading inn. In 1666 when Sir Richard Wynn was in London he wrote home saying he was much troubled at not hearing from his wife, adding that the drunkenness of the Denbigh postmaster 'will force him out of his place'. At this time Sir Richard was staying at the King's Head Tavern in Fleet Street. Lady Sara, in return, informed her husband that postmasters were very careless and that her letters had not arrived. While there seems to have been a postal service of a kind, some of the letters were carried by messengers. John Wynne of Melai asserts that a letter from Colonel Hugh Wynn had 'met with some rubs on the way'. There seems to have been a fairly regular postal service to Chester. A 'foot post' to Chester is mentioned by Sir John Wynn, the 5th Baronet, in Charles II reign:

'pray gette a petition drawn up to the post masters general in which sette properly forth how far we are at Llanrwst from a post town and as a trade begins to flourish to pray that they may allow 25 per annum so as to have a post three times a week from Denbigh with a horseman at Llanrwst, and let it be signed by as many gentlemen of the neighbourhood as you can and also the inhabitants of Llanrwst.'

Another note follows on 16 August: 'Send the petition for Llanrwst post office as soon as possible and also Mr Rice Williams certificate.' A draft for the petition drawn up by 'Gentleman in the post office' suggested the miles should be checked. There the correspondence ends. A note in pencil states: 'there was a foot post from Betws to Llanrwst in 1811 but the date of the opening is unknown.'

Formerly seven of the town's pillar-boxes were adorned with 'V R', indicative of their age. This conjures up a picture of sacks of mail carried in a red-painted 'mail-cart' with a fast trotting pony driven by a blue uniformed postman whose headgear shaped like a French kepi probably owes its design to the effect of the Franco-Prussian War of 1870.

The telegram-boy on a red bicycle is also a thing of the past. The pillar-box in the square suggested a likely place for an early post office until it was moved in 2002. One might hazard a guess that the establishment of a permanent post office coincided with the coming of the railway, which put Llanrwst in close touch with the Irish Mail. There is a map of Llanrwst in 1875, which marks a post office in the square. By 1828 there was a regular weekly parcels service from Chester to Llanrwst, writes Professor A H Dodd in his *History of Wrexham*, 1957.

THE RAILWAY

The railway line to Llanrwst played an important part in the town's development. So anxious were residents to secure the advantages it would bring that many signed a petition to Baroness de Eresby of Gwydir appealing for permission to allow the track to cross her lands. The petition on vellum is preserved in the office of Messrs Griffith and Griffith, agents to the Gwydir Estate.

The first sod was cut on ground which once formed part of the abbey of Aberconwy at Maenan on 27 August 1860. The ceremony was performed by Mr William Hanmer, MA, JP, of Bodnod Hall who was accompanied by his wife. They were presented with a silver gilt spade bearing the Hanmer coat-of-arms. In June 1960 the spade was sold at an auction of transport bric-a-brac in London for eighty pounds.

The line, which reached Blaenau Ffestiniog in 1879, was built in sections. The first portion to Llanrwst covered eleven and a half miles from the old station at the Junction. It was opened in 1863 as the 'Conwy to Llanrwst railway', which was taken over by the London and North Western Railway in 1867. The station is well-designed and neatly built as its artistic chimneys testify; testimony to Llanrwst's pride in its railway station. Hitherto all goods dispatched or received had to be conveyed in horse-drawn vehicles. The formation of the Llanrwst Agricultural Show in 1870 suggests the impetus which rail transport brought to an agricultural community.

An account published 8 September 1860 states that the act for the construction of the railway was obtained at the last session of parliament principally through the exertions of Edmund Sharpe Esq, of Coed-y-celyn, near Llanrwst, the chairman of the provisional directors. After mentioning the cutting of the first sod by William Hanmer Esq, of Bodnod, 'the principal landowner on the line, in the presence of a large concourse of persons of all ranks from all parts of the valley', the

account continues that the spade was of twisted oak with a blade of silver, inscribed and presented to Mr Hanmer by Mr Sharpe. Mr Sharpe then cut the next sod and was followed by H
Sandbach of Hafodunos Esq, R O Mousedale of Bryndyffryn Esq, H Spier Hughes Esq and
others and finally by Master Alfred Sharpe, son of the chairman. Among the numerous guests
were Admiral and Mrs Watling of Fron Ganol.

Other guests were Miss Naylor of Coedfa, Hugh Beaver Roberts Esq, Mr and Mrs Drabble of
Bron Derw, Mrs Darbishire, Pendyffryn, the Misses Anwyll Roberts, Careglleon, Rev J and Mrs
Morgan, Llandudno, Mr and Mrs Griffiths of Beaver Grove, Major Bird, Mr H Bird, Dr William
Hughes, Llanrwst, Mr and Mrs Beach, Gwydir Uchaf and Mr Brotherwood of Cilcennus. The
grounds of the abbey were then thrown open by Lord Newborough and dancing on the lawn was
kept up until a late hour.

A contemporary newspaper describes the opening of the line to Llanrwst in June 1863:

‘A special train left the Victoria Railway Station, Manchester, at eight o’ clock in the morning
carrying a number of ladies and gentlemen to take part in the ceremony of opening the
branch of the railway. At Chester and other stations invited guests were picked up and the
train deposited its visitors at Llandudno at noon. Half an hour was allowed for a ramble on
the beach and a scramble on the hill by the baths, then the train started for Llanrwst. The new
line crosses the Chester and Holyhead railway at the Llandudno and Conwy Junction and
then runs along the edge of the River Conwy.’

Cutting the first sod of the Conwy and Llanrwst Railway in 1860

Having stated that the cost of the line was seventy five thousand pounds and that it presented no engineering difficulty, the writer gives an enthusiastic description of the scenery:

'The train arrived at Llanrwst about half past one. Large numbers of people mustered about the station and yard and a band dressed in volunteer uniform gave a Welsh rendering of 'Rule Britannia'. Luncheon was served under a tent at the back of the Eagles Inn. About one hundred and forty sat down under the presidency of Mr Bancroft of Manchester. The party broke up about five and the return train left Llanrwst station in brilliant sunshine at six and arrived in Manchester at ten.'

DISTINGUISHED GUESTS

Following the Diamond Jubilee of Queen Victoria in 1897, the Earl of Carrington entertained three of the overseas Premiers – The Right Honourable Sir Wilfrid Laurier of Canada, the Right Honourable Richard Seddon of New Zealand and the Right Honourable G Reid, New South Wales. With them was Sir Lewis Davies, Canada's Minister of Marine. Lord and Lady Carrington took advantage of the occasion to arrange for their guests to visit Llanrwst where a crowd mustered in the Square to welcome them. Mr Elias was there and has preserved a photograph of Sir Wilfrid Laurier addressing the assembly.

A day's holiday was officially declared for the occasion and this practice followed two years later when Lord and Lady Carrington entertained at Gwydir the Duke and Duchess of York, later King George V and Queen Mary. Commemorative oaks were planted at Gwydir on this occasion and added to the trees already planted by distinguished guests.

Lord Carrington accompanied the Prince of Wales, later King Edward VII when he made a world tour in *H M S Seraphis*. Later the Earl purchased the furniture used by the Prince on that occasion and added it to Gwydir's historical collection thereby starting a rumour that King Edward once stayed there.

In 1920 Gwydir was bought by a well-known art dealer, Mr Duveen, and the contents were put up for auction. The castle was purchased by the Countess of Tankerville and many of the treasures were brought back and restored to their original places.

But disaster was impending and in July 1922 historic Gwydir was gutted by fire. The *North Wales Weekly News* of July 13 contains an account from which the following is extracted:

'Gwydir Castle, the beautiful and historic Tudor mansion located on the banks of the Conwy near Llanrwst and one of the most historical residences in North Wales, was destroyed by fire early on Sunday morning. It was first observed by P C Williams, Trefriw, who immediately made tracks for the castle, when he found that the caretaker, Mr Kennedy, had been alarmed and that the other occupant Countess Tankerville's mother, Mrs Vanderman, a lady advanced in years and her housekeeper were also safe'.

'The flames gained extraordinary fierceness in a very short time, for within a few minutes after the alarm, the whole of the eastern wing, containing the famous banqueting hall and Hall of Justice, was a mass of flames and it was very evident to all that this portion of the pile was doomed, so that the Llanrwst Fire Brigade when it arrived concentrated its efforts on the saving of the western wing........the destroyed portion of the castle contained some priceless objects of art........the banqueting hall was thrown open to visitors on the day of the recent fete and the evident enormous expenditure on this room was only matched by the exquisite taste her ladyship displayed in the arrangements. On Friday evening the Justice Hall had just been completed. Fires had been kept in the rooms and most probably to this the calamity will be traced. It is estimated her ladyship expended no less a sum than fifty thousand pounds in restoring the art treasures in this room.'

A second fire occurred not long after.

The property was purchased about 1944 by the late Mr Arthur Clegg, a retired bank manager and he and his wife devoted all their time to restoring the castle. Only those who saw Gwydir so soon after the fire can appreciate the magnitude of this self imposed task but the Gwydir of today is a monument to their memory. Mr Clegg found that the room above the great hall had, behind its ceiling, majestic hammer beams and massive timbers. He stripped the ceiling and the woodwork and the original roof was revealed, doubtless as it came from the abbey at Maenan. Several fireplaces had older fireplaces behind them; in one instance a low doorway gave access to a secret chamber.

In 1555 (the date on the Gwydir gateway) a list of ministers includes the name of 'John Wynne Meredithe, Esquire, Steward of the Lord King and Lady Queen of the Monastery of Conwy'. The document is in the Caernarvonshire Record Office – *Catalogue of Quarter Sessions Rolls. MS68.*

ADMIRAL JOHN WYATT WATLING

In the neglected burial ground of St Mary's Church lies a brave naval officer who fought through the Napoleonic Wars before retiring to Llanrwst. His actual adventures resemble those depicted in the sea stories of Captain Marryat as he fought French frigates in any part of the world where he could find the tricolour flying.

In Llanrwst there appears to be little known of him apart from an epitaph and his name bestowed upon a road which caused visitors to marvel that the Romans extended their famous highway as far as Llanrwst! His death appears to have passed unnoticed locally save for a modest obituary in the *North Wales Chronicle* of 30 November 1867:

'On the 28 inst…, at his residence, Fronganol near Llanrwst, Admiral John Wyatt Watling in the 81st year of his age.'

Born in Leominster of a family descended from Sir Thomas Wyatt Watling, he went to sea as a boy in the merchant service, but on account of the war situation he transferred to the Royal Navy and on 4 March 1801 he signed on as an 'ordinary' on board *HMS Veteran*. In a few days time the ship joined the fleet in the expedition against Copenhagen. When on 2nd April the British attacked the Danish forts and batteries, Wyatt, aged fourteen, was one of the crew of the *Veteran's* cutter which reported for duty at Nelson's flagship, the *Elephant*.

He was still in the midst of a terrible bombardment, which caused two British seventy-fours to run aground, so dense was the battlesmoke. Watling's cutter was one which assisted in rendering assistance to the *Bellons* and *Russel,* which had grounded. The boat then helped to tow the shattered *Monarch* out of action.

He then took possession of several prizes. His conduct obviously attracted attention for he was made a midshipman, continuing to serve in the *Veteran* until June the following year when he was transferred to the *Acasta* and sailed for the Mediterranean. In the *Goliath* he aided……..'in cutting out a French brig from under the protection of a national cutter of ten guns and of the powerful batteries at Sable d' Olonne'.

While belonging to the *Virginia,*which ship was stationed chiefly off the coast of Ireland, Mr Watling contributed to the capture on 10 May 1809 of the Dutch frigate *Guelderland* of thirty six guns and two hundred and fifty men after an obstinate conflict of an hour and a half………on leaving *Virginia* he was nominated, having just passed his examination, Acting Lieutenant of the *Hero*. He was confirmed 22nd September 1808 and on the 22 of the following month he was appointed to the *Sirius* under Capt Sam Pym. Proceeding in her to the Cape station, Mr Watling was afforded an opportunity, 21 September 1809, of assisting at the capture of the town of St Pauls in the Ile de Bourbon, on which occasion the *Sirius* stood in the harbour, anchored within half-musket shot of *La Caroline*, a French frigate, two prize Indiamen and a brig-of-war and opened so heavy a fire that in twenty minutes the whole of them struck their colours.

In June 1610, we find Mr Watling commanding the pinnace, in company with the other boats of the *Sirius* under Lieut Wm Norman and displaying conduct that did him great credit, in a successful attack on a deeply-laden three-masted schooner, which the enemy had run aground in a creek near Port Louis in Mauritius, within two hundred yards of the shore. It was under protection of about three hundred troops and several strong batteries. In face of all the opposition that could be made the vessel was boarded and burnt.

When preparations were made for the subjugation of the Ile de Bourbon, it is stated that Mr Watling was entrusted with the duty of superintending the debarkation of the whole of the troops, in number nine hundred and fifty……. 'and in such an astonishing fine style' to use the words of Capt Pym, did he and the seaman under him perform their part that in less than two hours and a half that entire body was landed safely and on the march despite the heavy surf and rolling-stone beach. He next assisted in the storming and capture of the Ile de la Passe. On the death of the lieutenant in charge Mr Watling took command of the party landed by the *Sirius* and was warmly recommended for his conduct by the Commander-in-Chief.

Another exploit was to capture a thirty-gun French vessel with two boats of British seamen armed with nothing but the boats' stretchers. On another occasion when his vessel with several others was trapped by a French squadron it was resolved to set fire to the ships.

He was employed in a boat conveying to the different ships the instructions of Capt Pym, the senior officer, and when it became necessary to destroy the Sirius to prevent her falling into the hands of the enemy, he nearly lost his life through his intrepidity in going below, after she had been abandoned, and in opening the magazine doors, in order that the flames which had been kindled might the more readily communicate to it and accomplish the object in view.

As soon as the frigate had been blown up he volunteered to convey Capt Pym's dispatches in an open boat to the Ile de Bourbon a distance of one hundred and forty miles; on his arrival there he was presented by Governor Farquhar with the sum of two hundred pounds and sent in the *Egremont*, a prize schooner fitted for the purpose, to Madras with intelligence of the disasters which had occurred. After enduring many hardships he reached Madras, where in acknowledgement of the services he had rendered to the East India Company, he had the gratification of receiving from the Governor General in Council a further sum of two hundred pounds!

The following year, after receiving a strong letter of recommendation, he was sent with dispatches to the island of Rodrigues but had to be sent to sick quarters because the fatigue he had undergone had so reduced his health.

'The Commander-in-Chief, Vice-Admiral Bertie, on this occasion publicly expressed to him on the quarterdeck of his flagship, the Africaine the regret he felt.' Whilst recuperating at Bourbon he was appointed governor of the port. He was later sent to Mauritius where the governor placed him in command of a large American prize schooner and sent him home with dispatches:

'Prior to his departure for England he had the good fortune, in a four-oared gig, to rescue from apparent inevitable destruction the wife of the major in the army and fifteen other persons who had been wrecked on a coral reef near Port Louis in a vessel over which the waves were dashing in awful fury. The devoted heroism he displayed in achieving this act of humanity was witnessed by thousands of persons from the shore and had the effect of drawing an eulogium from the governor.'

After service in home waters he was sent in the *Minden* to the Cape of Good Hope and advanced to the rank of commander on 1st December 1813. His last command on active service was the *Julia*, one of the watch vessels of St Helena during Napoleon's imprisonment. Having been invalided home he was appointed Inspecting Commander of the Coastguard until he retired on half pay with the rank of captain on 22nd July 1830.

This occurred but a few weeks after the death of his first wife who was a daughter of Philip Grubbm of Highgate. When and why he came to Llanrwst is not known. He married his second wife Martha Hughes, eldest daughter of Peter Titler, DL surgeon and apothecary, of Pen-loyn, Llanrwst. They made their home at Fron-ganol, then a remote place on the slopes to the east of the town. During his naval activities Admiral Watling had been severely wounded in the right hand so that two fingers were rendered useless. He played a prominent part in local life being a Justice of the Peace for Denbighshire and Caernarvonshire and a Deputy Lieutenant for the latter county. The admiral's epitaph in the now demolished Church of St Mary read:-

Sacred
to the memory of
ADMIRAL
John Wyatt Watling
of Fron Ganol
Born April 9 1787

Also of
Martha Hughes Watling
his beloved wife
Born March 21 1802
Died February 23 1877.

Fron-ganol is marked on the tithe map of 1844. The admiral designed a new house for himself, its original incorporating nautical features.

LLANRWST
AND DISTRICT
IN PHOTOGRAPHS

Above: The former Town Hall adjacent to the Pen-y-Bryn Hotel

Left: W. J. William's shop at Regent House, on the corner of the Ancaster Square, 1905

Market day with stalls offering wares and with ladies browsing and no doubt looking for a bargain. They were taken in 1909 (above) and 1905 (below)

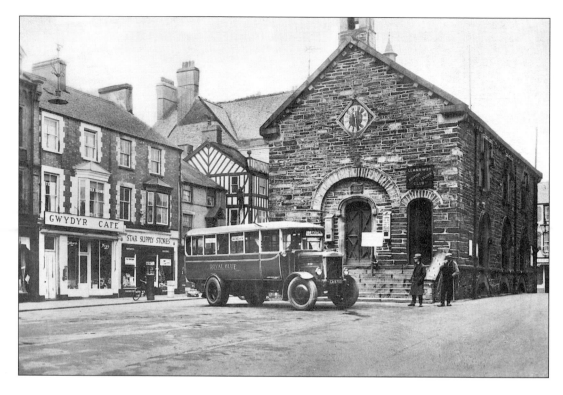

Two more views of Ancaster Square

Above: A busier market day scene with the same two covered stalls as on page 62
Below: A piano accordianist with amused on lookers in Denbigh Street, 1907

A fascinating scene outside the George & Dragon
Vaults in 1912. The rear sign says "Carriages for hire"
Below: The Cattle Fair in Denbigh Street on a rainy day in 1909

Above: The staff of E. P. Jones, Son & Co, butchers and grocers, 1907
Below: Looking from Denbigh Street to what is now the HSBC Bank premises in Ancaster Square

Above: A tranquil scene in Station Road
Below: The Llanrwst and Trefriw Railway Station

Two views in Station Road, taken from the same position, one in winter and the other in summer

Two further views of Station Road

Bridge Street: Looking towards the bridge (above) and towards Ancaster Square (below)

Above: The fair in 1909 in Ancaster Square
Below: The visit of the future King George V and Queen Mary to Gwydir Castle in 1899

Above: This remarkable photograph shows the building which was replaced by the Midland Bank (now HSBC) and the former King's Head pub, now the British Legion. It was taken prior to 1870
Below: The Eagles Hotel and the parish church

Two views of the former Victoria Hotel, one of the town's most elegant buildings

The bridge and Victoria Hotel, looking upriver

Above: Gower's Bridge in Edwardian times
Below: The former Toll House on the corner of School Bank Road and the road to Betws-y-coed

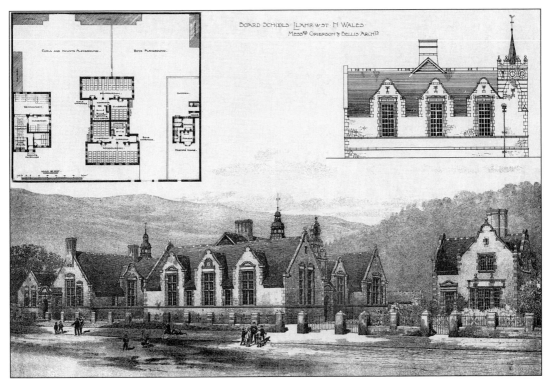

Above: The architect's drawing for the new school buildings, School Bank Road. From *Building News*, June 1896
Below: An Edwardian photograph of the then County School

Above: The Seion Chapel, off Station Road
Below: St James Methodist Chapel

Two views of the former St Mary's Church

Above: Interior of the Chapel at Llanrhychwyn   Below: The Tabernacl Church in Parry Road

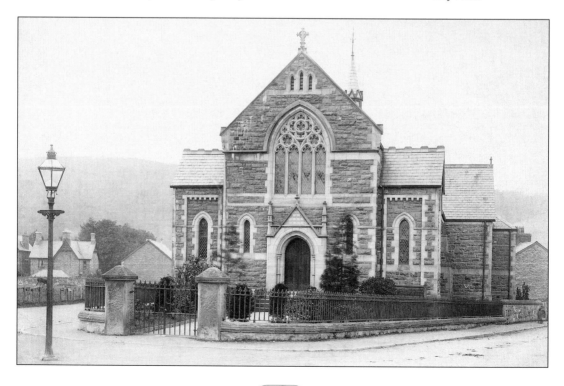

Above: A scene in Nebo
Below: The staff of the Cae Coch Pyrites Mine, 1882. Some of the men have their shovels, hammers or riddles with them

Above: Children from the Llanrwst Council School. The photograph is not dated
Below: An early photograph of the police department

The river steamer from Conwy. It was paddle-wheel driven

GWYDIR CASTLE

Left: The castle's
imposing entrance
Below: The castle
entrance gate

Peacocks and peahens compliment the tranquility of the gardens (see over)

Four views from the garden

Above: The Drawing Room   Below: The Dining Room
Opposite page; Top: The State Bedroom   Below: Gwydir Woods

TREFRIW

Above: The view towards the Woollen Mill
Below: The garage with its "new fangled" petrol pumps would be of little interest to this gentleman and his nicely turned-out trap

Above: The slate quay in 1857, thought to have been taken by Roger Fenton. Note the ship being loaded
Below: Quieter days on the quay

Above: The steamer service to and from Conwy used to be very popular
Below: A quiet day on the main road through the village

Above: There is a lot of interest in this view of the village shops and the former Geirionydd Hotel, now
The Fairy Falls Hotel. Notice the horse and cart and what appears to be a thatched hay rick
Below: The Post Office and Post Office Savings Bank. The Garage sign advertises cars for hire

Above: A close up of the properties in the background of the last photograph in 1909. Notice the barrels on the left

Below: The village in 1910. The sign is for the Rhianva apartments which also offered teas and also carried the CTC (Cyclists Touring Club) logo

Above: Trefriw village
Below: Lazy summer holidays by the bridge

Above: Trefriw village c. 1930s
Below: The Hotel Belle Vue

Two views of Trefriw
Chalybeate Wells

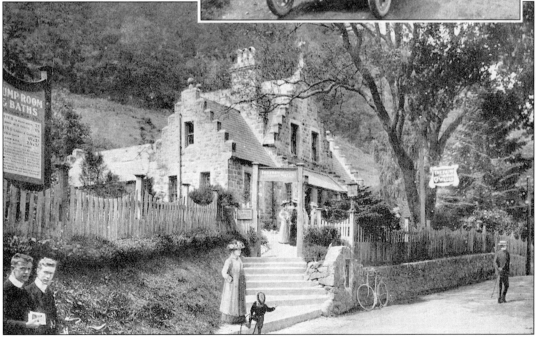

Visitors to the Spa. (above & below) The above view shows the Pump Room and the doorway to the Ladies Baths

TREFRIW CHALYBEATE WELLS.

ANCIENT CAVE
OF THE WELLS.

SHEWING THE HILL-SIDE ENTRANCE
AND THE ROCK-HEWN BASINS IN
WHICH THE WATERS ARE COLLECTED,
WHENCE THEY ARE CONDUCTED TO
THE PUMPROOM, BATHS AND THE
BOTTLING DEPARTMENT

Above: This photograph is endorsed "Living waxworks, 1905"

Opposite page: The Flannel Mills of Thomas Williams and Son

Opposite page;
Views of the former Parc
Mine which was worked
for lead. The mine
conveyor, carrying
crushed ore (top left) and
mine cars, one of which is
on a tipper and being
emptied (bottom) The
other is of cars leaving
the No. 3 level

This page;
Top: A rock drill in use
Middle: The floation cells
for extracting fine particles
of ore
Bottom: The entrance
to the No. 3 level

LLANRWST TODAY

9

Above: Bridge Street   Below: Watling Street

Above: Station Road   Below: Watling Street

Two views of the Parish Church gates

Opposite page; Top: Ysgol Dyffryn Conwy
Bottom: Ysgol Brogwydir

The Parish Church

Pen-y-Bryn Hotel (left) and the Eagles Hotel (above). Hidden behind its layer of creeper is the Tu-hwnt-i'r-bont tearooms

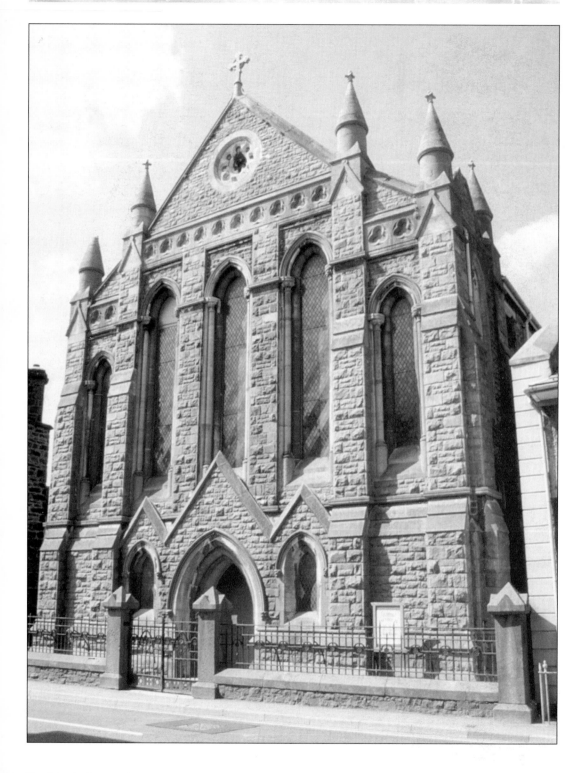

The Horeb Chapel, Station Road

Above left: The Welsh Presbyterian or Seion Chapel
Above right: The Llanrwst Institute
Below: The Old Tannery

INDEX

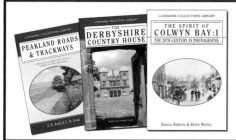
Mining Histories
- Collieries of South Wales: Vol 1   *ISBN: 1 84306 015 9, £22.50*
- Collieries of South Wales: Vol 2   *ISBN: 1 84306 017 5, £19.95*
- Collieries of Somerset & Bristol   *ISBN: 1 84306 029 9, £14.95*
- Copper & Lead Mines around the Manifold Valley, North Staffordshire   *ISBN: 1 901522 77 6, £19.95*
- Images of Cornish Tin   *ISBN: 1 84306 020 5, £29.95*
- Lathkill Dale, Derbyshire, its Mines and Miners   *ISBN: 1 901522 80 6, £8.00*
- Rocks & Scenery the Peak District   *ISBN: 1 84306 026 4, paperback, £7.95*
- Swaledale, its Mines & Smelt Mills   *ISBN: 1 84306 018 3, £19.95*

Industrial Histories
- Alldays and Onions   *ISBN: 1 84306 047 7, £24.95*
- The Life & Inventions of Richard Roberts, 1789 -1864   *ISBN: 1 84306 027 2, £29.95*
- The Textile Mill Engine   *ISBN: 1 901522 43 1, paperback, £22.50*
- Watt, James, His Life in Scotland, 1736-74   *ISBN 1 84306 045 0, £29.95*
- Wolseley, The Real, Adderley Park Works, 1901-1926   *ISBN 1 84306 052 3, £19.95*
- Morris Commercial   *ISBN: 1 84306 069 8 (Price to be announced)*

Roads & Transportantion
- Packmen, Carriers & Packhorse Roads   *ISBN: 1 84306 016 7, £19.95*
- Roads & Trackways of Wales   *ISBN: 1 84306 019 1, £22.50*
- Welsh Cattle Drovers   *ISBN: 1 84306 021 3, £22.50*
- Peakland Roads & Trackways   *ISBN: 1 901522 91 1, £19.95*

Regional/Local Histories
- Colwyn Bay, Its History across the Years   *ISBN: 1 84306 014 0, £24.95*
- Crosses of the Peak District   *ISBN 1 84306 044 2, £14.95*
- Derbyshire Country Houses: Vol 1   *ISBN: 1 84306 007 8, £19.95*
- Derbyshire Country Houses: Vol 2   *ISBN: 1 84306 041 8, £19.95*
- Historic Hallamshire   *ISBN: 1 84306 049 3, £19.95*
- Llandudno: Queen of Welsh Resorts   *ISBN 1 84306 048 5, £15.95*
- Llanrwst: the History of a Market Town   *ISBN 1 84306 070 1, £14.95*
- Lost Houses in and around Wrexham   *ISBN 1 84306 057 4, £16.95*
- Lost Houses of Derbyshire   *ISBN: 1 84306 064 7, £19.95, October 02*
- Shipwrecks of North Wales   *ISBN: 1 84306 005 1, £19.95*
- Shrovetide Football and the Ashbourne Game   *ISBN: 1 84306 063 9, £19.95*
- Well Dressing   *ISBN: 1 84306 042 6, Full colour, £19.95*